To my wife, Sharon, and daughters
Clarissa and Peggy Anne

Wilderness Canoeing & Camping

Wilderness Canoeing & Camping

Cliff Jacobson

A Sunrise Book   E. P. DUTTON   NEW YORK

The author expresses special thanks to the following:

Backpacking Journal (Spring 1977) for permission to reprint, in its entirety, his article "Canoeing with Children" (which appears in Chapter 8 as "Tripping with Tots and Teens").
Backpacker Magazine (#13, February 1976) for permission to use portions of his article "Compass Evaluations."
Blair and Ketchum's *Country Journal* (July 1975) for permission to use material from his article "Canoe Camping on a Shoestring."
Canoe magazine for use of their *1975–76 Buyer's Guide,* and as a source.
Oar & Paddle magazine (July–August 1974) for permission to use his article "Are You in Love with Your Canoe Paddle?"

Library of Congress Cataloging in Publication Data

Jacobson, Cliff.
  Wilderness canoeing & camping.

  "A Sunrise book."
  1. Canoes and canoeing. 2. Camping.   I. Title.
GV789.J32   1977   797.1'22   76-24463

ISBN: 0-87690-228-X (cloth)
      0-87690-229-8 (paper)

Published simultaneously in Canada by Clarke, Irwin & Company Limited, Toronto and Vancouver

10 9 8 7 6 5 4 3 2

Contents

Acknowledgments

Special thanks should be extended to:

My friend Marc Hebert, for his advice and patient reading of the manuscript.

Bob O'Hara and Bob Dannert, for their advice on arctic canoe travel.

Betty Ketter, for her information on the history of canoe racing and strip canoe building.

Verlen Kruger, for supplying information about his canoe voyage to the Bering Sea.

My friend Paul Swanstrom, for his design and drawings of the canoe cover and its fittings.

Mark Lindbeck, my talented and patient photographer.

Al Button, one of America's top white-water canoe competitors, for his information on modern paddling technique.

Norma Meutzel and John Gabriel, for their help in punctuating the manuscript.

Ken Saelens, for the photos of his canoe tumpline invention.

Bob Gramprie and Paul Johnston of the Sawyer Canoe Company, for their information on canoe design and fiberglass canoe construction.

The Minnesota Canoe Association and U.S. Canoe Association, for their information on strip canoe building.

The manufacturers of canoes and paddles whose names appear in the appendix, for their product information and photographs.

A
Note to
the Reader

In the process of writing this book I came to realize that expounding my canoe philosophy was a lot like trying to tell someone what constitutes good art. Naturally I believe that my way is the best way, but there are a lot of equally knowledgeable canoeists who would disagree. I've found that if you want to get along with other paddlers, you'd better keep an open mind. You can easily get into a hassle over what constitutes the best canoe tent, the most comfortable footwear, the most waterproof way to pack for a wilderness trip, and so on. Often what works for one canoeist won't work for another. For example, I prefer lightweight, rubber-bottom, leather-top boots for canoeing. But I weigh only 135 pounds, so this type of footgear works fine for me. A friend of mine weighs 240 pounds; he went through a pair of similar boots in just four weeks, on one canoe trip.

The type of wilderness experiences a canoeist has also influences his or her methods. If you've ever tipped over and had your canoe swept under a submerged tree, there to remain until low water sets it free, you might be very much opposed to tying your gear in the canoe. But if your canoe and outfit have been saved because of the extra buoyancy of tightly lashed packs, then you may be a real believer in tying *everything* in.

Thus the equipment and methods which I recommend are the result of my experiences and those of others whom I know personally or have contacted. I am continually revising my ideas of what is best. Possibly by the time you read this I will already consider some of my recommendations outdated. If you take canoeing seriously (or plan to), you should read every canoe book in print—not once, but many times. Only after you have studied the works of others—and paddled many miles—will you know what is best for you. I won't pretend that this book is a complete treatise on canoeing. It's not; no single book could be. But hopefully you'll find some worthwhile hints contained within these pages.

CLIFF JACOBSON

Hastings, Minnesota
September 1976

Wilderness Canoeing & Camping

1.
The Wilderness Challenge

It is difficult to pinpoint what makes canoeing so attractive a pastime. The inexpensiveness of the sport attracts some, and the thrills of competition lure others. For me it is the wilderness challenge. Many of the really wild places in North America are easily accessible only by canoe, and even in the most crowded cities there is always a little-used river which can be floated to get away from it all. But a canoe is more than wilderness transportation and white-water excitement. It is a tonic for tedium and a unique form of family therapy—togetherness. The green revolution, the ecology movement, a suffering economy, and too much war have all contributed to the popularity of canoeing. Americans are at last becoming reattuned to nature. We are trading in our Vanbagos for nylon tents and hiking boots; we are rediscovering the wilderness.

But the wilderness has changed. It is becoming increasingly difficult to find places to be alone—places which do not show the scars of man. Virtually all of the great northern rivers are now paddled regularly. Even in the arctic it is unusual to travel for weeks at a time in complete

1

isolation from other human beings or evidence of them. If our wild places are to survive the brunt of the thousands who are returning to nature, we must do more than provide lip service to the modern wilderness ethic; leave only footprints, take only pictures. And that is the beauty of the canoe: not even footprints are left. For this reason canoeists are more fortunate than backpackers. We don't have to look at mile after mile of littered, eroded trails and crowded or nonexistent campsites. We can simply pitch a tent on a passing sandbar and time will eliminate any trace of our presence.

Nevertheless, the environmental crisis is here—for the canoeist as well as the backpacker. During the past decade canoeing has grown so popular that today well over a hundred manufacturers find a profitable livelihood in the production of more than seven hundred canoe and kayak models. New designs, materials, and construction methods have resulted in canoes which are lighter, faster, and tougher than anything the Indians ever built. Canoe-tripping equipment has changed, too. Tents, sleeping bags, cooking gear—everything has become lighter, stronger, and more compact. As a result, thousands of new paddlers are taking to our waterways each year. Already the impact of these canoeists is being felt upon the wildness of the wilderness.

Although lightweight equipment and new techniques have significantly reduced the risks of canoe trips in isolated areas, your most important skill on a difficult venture is still your own good judgment. Many significant canoe voyages have been successfully completed by relatively incompetent canoeists. That these individuals survived can best be attributed to their good sense in portaging a set of complex rapids rather than dashing heedlessly downstream for a quick and final ego trip.

In 1930 Eric Sevareid, the noted news commentator, and Walter Port paddled from Minneapolis, Minnesota, to Hudson Bay via the Gods River. No white person had ever completed this trip and neither Eric nor Tom had much canoeing or camping experience. They survived the hazardous journey because of their cool and accurate appraisal of dangerous situations and a portage-rather-than-perish attitude.

Only the foolhardy will take unnecessary risks which endanger their lives. Every modern canoe club has a few of these carefree individuals, and some of them are excellent paddlers. Such persons should, for your own safety, be left out of your wilderness trip plans. Don't think you have to be an Olympic canoeist to undertake a voyage of significance. Of course you need skill and the right gear, but mostly you need to keep your wits about you.

Most canoes have excellent resale value, even when they are many years old. If you are on a limited budget and can afford to buy an inexpensive canoe now, you can work your way up to a better model within a few years with little financial loss. As you paddle you will gain experience and learn more efficient ways to camp and canoe. When you are ready for a really fine canoe, you will have developed the knowledge and skill to appreciate it and you will damage it less in difficult waters because your apprenticeship will have been served.

Because the canoe is such a versatile and wonderful craft, it deserves your study if you are to derive the greatest benefits from its use. Loaded and handled properly, a well-designed canoe will ride out running waves that would frighten most powerboaters. And the same canoe that can carry you hundreds of miles across wilderness waters will drift quietly along peaceful local rivers, filled with kids and dogs and coolers, providing you and your family with an inexpensive and enjoyable way to discover nature.

2.
The Wilderness
Canoe—
An Investment
in Freedom

With so many manufacturers making canoes, you would think there'd be hundreds of models suitable for wilderness canoeing. There aren't. To most people a canoe is a canoe, and this, compounded by the fact that most canoe builders are not canoeists, keeps the sales of badly designed, poorly constructed models booming. Many are merely producing a popular product at an attractive price. Even the powerboater fares better in this respect, for when he goes to a marina to buy a new or used craft, the salesman has at least some idea of what makes a good speedboat. Few canoe salespeople have ever paddled the canoes they sell, fewer own canoes, and almost none have ever taken a serious wilderness trip in one. They will, however, appear very knowledgeable, especially when you are about to part with your money. So canoe selection is pretty much up to the buyer, and the old economic adage *caveat emptor* ("let the buyer beware") really applies here, for there are some really bad canoes on the market. Evidently ignorance begets ignorance, for even if you make a bad choice, the high demand for canoes will prevent you from getting hurt very much. Even the worst of the commercial canoes can probably be sold for sixty percent of its original purchase price five years later—providing, of course, it has been well kept. There is an antithesis here. Most people are so ignorant about canoes that if you invest in a *really* good one you may find the resale potential extremely limited. For example, in 1973 I organized a trip to James Bay, Ontario. One of my canoes, a white-water model, was too specialized for the trip, and the other, a fiberglass 17′9″ Sawyer, was too small for the big rapids and heavy loads we would be carrying. So I decided to trade the $275 Sawyer on a more suitable wilderness canoe. The best offer I could get from a marina was $125; I was advised that people didn't want "cheap plastic canoes." I pointed out that my Sawyer was not a cheap plastic canoe but a sophisticated cruiser with racing aspirations. "No matter," was the reply, "fiberglass is fiberglass." Ultimately, I advertised the canoe in *HUT*, the official publication of the Minnesota Canoe Association. The Sawyer went at $220 to a knowledgeable canoeist in less than a week after the ad appeared!

What kind of canoe should you buy and how much should you spend? Your choice depends on where and how you will use it. No one automobile will do everything well, and neither will a single canoe. If you plan to use a canoe for white-water sport as well as lake cruising and serious wilderness tripping, you may want two canoes. If you can afford only one, then you must carefully select a model which will do reasonably well in all categories. Finding such a canoe is difficult, although not impossible.

Before discussing construction materials and design features, you need to know some basic terminology.

CANOE TERMINOLOGY

Aft: Toward the stern (back) end of the canoe.

Amidships: The center or middle of the canoe.

Bailer: A scoop (usually made from an empty bleach jug by cutting off the bottom) for dipping accumulated water from the bottom of the canoe.

Bang plate: On aluminum canoes. A curved metal plate running from deck to keel. Holds the metal skin together and takes the bangs. The bang plate is called the *stem band* on canoes of wood-canvas construction.

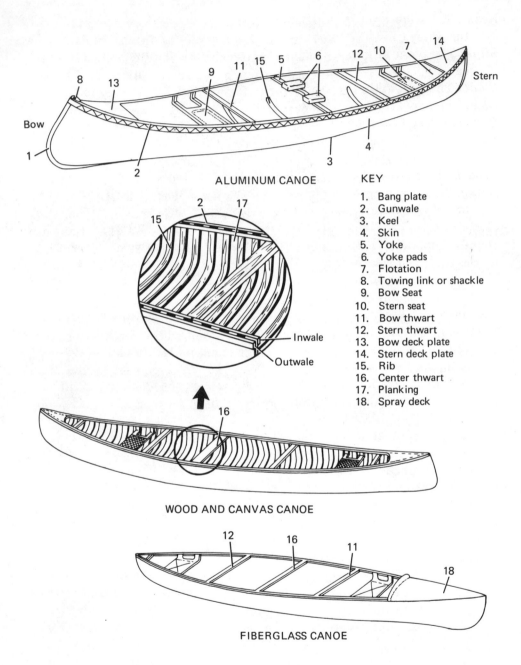

ALUMINUM CANOE

Bow

Stern

KEY

1. Bang plate
2. Gunwale
3. Keel
4. Skin
5. Yoke
6. Yoke pads
7. Flotation
8. Towing link or shackle
9. Bow Seat
10. Stern seat
11. Bow thwart
12. Stern thwart
13. Bow deck plate
14. Stern deck plate
15. Rib
16. Center thwart
17. Planking
18. Spray deck

Inwale

Outwale

WOOD AND CANVAS CANOE

FIBERGLASS CANOE

FIGURE 1.

Beam: The widest part of the canoe. Generally occurs at or slightly aft of the waist (middle) and just below the gunwales.

Bilge: The point of greatest curvature between the bottom and side of a canoe.

Blade: The part of the canoe paddle that is placed in the water.

Bow: The forward (front) end of the canoe.

Bowman: The forward or bow paddler (whether male or female).

Broadside: A canoe which is perpendicular to the current of a river, thus exposing its broad side to obstacles in the water.

Broach: To turn suddenly into the wind.

Carry: To carry a canoe and gear overland, either to a distant watershed or to safer water. *Carry* is synonymous with *portage.*

Deck: Panels at the bow and stern which attach to the gunwales.

Depth: The distance from the top of the gunwales to the bottom of the canoe when measured at the beam (sometimes called *center depth,* as opposed to the depth at the extreme ends of the canoe).

Draft: The amount of water a canoe displaces.

Flat water: Water without rapids, such as a lake or slow-moving river.

Flotation: Styrofoam or other buoyant material set into the ends, along the inside bilges, or beneath the decks and gunwales of aluminum and fiberglass canoes to make them float if upset. Can also mean any buoyant material, such as life jackets, beach balls, and innertubes.

Fore (forward) : Toward the front end (bow) of the canoe.

Freeboard: The distance from the water line to the top of the gunwales at their lowest point. The greater the freeboard, the greater the ability of the canoe to handle rough water, assuming the canoe is well designed.

Grip: The top end of the shaft of a canoe paddle, where you grip it.

Gunwales (pronounced "gunnels") : The upper rails of the canoe.

Hogged: A canoe with a bent-in keel.

Inwale: That part of the gunwale that protrudes into the inside of the canoe.

Keel: A strip of wood or aluminum which runs along the center bottom of the canoe. Keels prevent lateral slippage in winds and protect the bottoms of canoes from damage in rocky areas. There are two types of keels in common use:

STANDARD, FIN, OR TEE KEEL

A deep keel which extends up to an inch or more into the water. An ideal choice where travel will be limited to large, windy lakes.

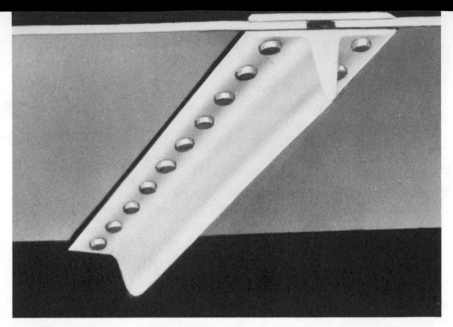

FIGURE 2. *Grumman Canoe Keels*
2a. Standard or Tee keels help prevent sideslipping on windy lakes.

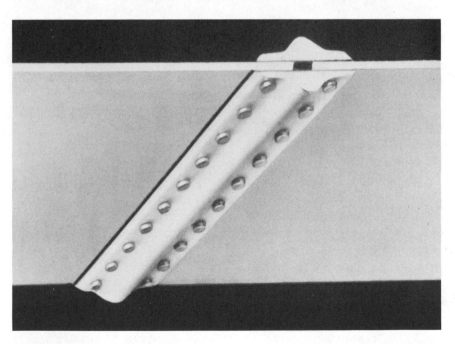

2b. Canoes with shallow draft shoe keels are more maneuverable and are less likely to catch on subsurface rocks than similar models with standard keels. (*Photos courtesy of Grumman Co.*)

SHOE (WHITE-WATER) KEEL
A rounded or flat strip of metal or wood designed to protect the bottom of a canoe from damage. The smooth contours of shoe keels allow water to flow over them with little resistance. Hence they permit quick turns in rapids.

Leeward: A sheltered or protected place out of the wind. In nautical terms, *leeward* is the direction toward which the wind is blowing.

Line: Rope used to tie up a canoe or pull it around obstacles in the water. Also refers to working a canoe downstream around obstacles in the water with the aid of ropes (lines) attached to the bow and stern.

Outwale: The part of the gunwale that protrudes over the outside of the canoe hull. Outwales are desirable for canoes that will be used in white water, as they help deflect spray when the bow of the canoe plunges in rapids.

Painters: Lines attached to the bow and stern of a canoe.

Planking: Lightweight boards nailed to the ribs on wood-canvas canoes. Planking runs perpendicular to the ribs of a canoe. Its main purpose is to support the canvas.

Portage: see *carry*.

Ribs: The lateral supports which run at right angles to the keel on the inside of a canoe. Ribs provide hull rigidity and structural strength, and are necessary on aluminum and wood-canvas canoes. The trend is away from ribs in canoes of modern construction, as the new synthetics are very strong and do not require cross-bracing for support.

Rocker: An upward curve of the keel line of a canoe. When placed on a level surface a canoe with rocker will, like a rocking chair, rock up and down (fore and aft). Canoes with rocker turn more easily than those without rocker.

Rock garden: A shallow place in a river that has many scattered rocks.

Seats: Generally, there are two seats in a canoe. They may be made of wood, fiberglass, plastic, or aluminum. Wood-framed seats which are strung with cane or nylon webbing and tractor-type molded fiberglass seats are most comfortable. Aluminum seats are least comfortable and get cold in cool weather. For greatest warmth (and comfort), cover aluminum seats with waterproof foam and secure the foam to the seats with waterproof tape. You spend long hours sitting in a canoe; consequently, more than passing consideration should be given to the seats.

Skin: The outer covering of the canoe. May be wood, canvas, aluminum, or other material.

Splash cover: A fitted cover designed to keep water out of a canoe. Splash covers are useful in rough rapids and big waves. Even small, sporty canoes are suitable for wilderness use if they are covered.

Spray deck: An extra-long deck equipped with a cowling to deflect water which comes over the ends of a canoe.

Spray skirt: A waterproof fabric sleeve which is attached to the splash cover at one end and is secured around a paddlers waist by means of elastic shock cord at the other end.

Thwart: A cross-brace which runs from gunwale to gunwale. Thwarts give strength and rigidity to the canoe's hull.

Tracking: Working a canoe upstream, against the current, with the aid of ropes (lines) attached to the bow and stern.

Trim: The difference in the draft at the bow from that at the stern of a canoe. A properly trimmed canoe will sit dead level in the water. Trim can be adjusted by weighting the bow or the stern.

Tumpline: A strap which is secured just above a person's forehead to help support a pack or canoe.

Waist: The middle of the canoe.

Water line: The place to which the water comes on the hull of the canoe when it is set in the water.

White water: Foamy (air-filled), turbulent water.

Yoke: A special crossbar equipped with shoulder pads for portaging the canoe.

SELECTING THE WILDERNESS CANOE

Wilderness canoes should be longer and deeper than those used for recreational paddling. Long canoes are faster (and thus easier to paddle) than short canoes, and deep hulls provide a margin of safety on wind-lashed lakes and thrashing rapids. Choose a canoe at least 17 feet long; 18 or 18½ feet is better. The width (beam) should be at least 34 inches, and the center depth not less than 13½ inches. (You can trade some beam and depth for length if your canoe is longer than 18 feet.) The bow, especially, should retain some fullness (width) right to the end so that it will have sufficient buoyancy to climb up over big standing waves and rollers without knifing dangerously through them.

Because a canoe's ability to rise and fall easily with waves depends upon its hull design and not the height of its ends, high bows and sterns serve little purpose other than to add weight to the canoe. Generally, ends should not be higher than the center depth of the canoe plus 10 inches. Thus, a canoe with a 13-inch depth should have a *maximum* end height of 23 inches. Ends that are too high act as sails, making canoe-handling on windblown lakes difficult.

KEELS—FRIEND OR FIEND?

Keels are the subject of much debate among experienced canoeists. Lake paddlers prefer keels up to 1½ inches deep, for canoes so equipped are easy to keep on course in a cross-wind. River canoeists, on the other hand, consider keels a fiendish device, as they are always catching on submerged rocks and logs. Also, keeled canoes are harder to turn than similar keelless models.

It would seem that you need *two* canoes for wilderness tripping— one for lakes, the other for rivers. But since you can paddle only one canoe at a time, a compromise craft must be found which incorporates the features of both lake and river canoes into its design. Such a compromise can be achieved by selecting a keelless canoe with a fairly straight bottom line. A straight bottom performs the same function as a keel, but will not catch on rocks. However, if a canoe's bottom is too straight, the craft won't turn readily, and this is a decided disadvantage in rapids, where quick turns are necessary. The solution is to build a slight upward curve or *rocker* into the keel line of the canoe. The greater the rocker, the easier the canoe will turn.

When I first became interested in white-water canoeing, I traded my standard, keeled aluminum canoe for a very responsive keelless model with a great deal of rocker. I took my wife on her first wilderness trip in this canoe. All went well until we encountered some very heavy, wind-driven waves. I told Sharon it was unsafe to continue, but she insisted on reaching a certain distant campsite whose virtues I had extolled. To keep water out of the canoe, I began striking the waves at a slight angle, but my strength was not enough to hold the skittish canoe on course. We swung broadside, gulping several inches of water. Luckily

I brought the canoe around in time to avoid another large wave. Sluggishly we paddled to an island to dump the accumulated water. Sharon blamed the entire episode on me; I, of course, blamed the canoe.

Fiberglass, ABS plastic, and wood canoes can all be had with fairly straight bottoms and no keels. Aluminum models, however, are stamped and formed in two pieces and riveted together at the keel line, so keels are essential. Many aluminum-canoe makers are now providing, on special order and at extra cost, shallow-draft *shoekeels* (figure 2) in place of the standard fin type normally furnished. Aluminum canoes with shoe keels handle very nicely in white water, but most, due to high buoyancy of their hulls and excessive rocker, are too skittish for use on windy lakes. This skittishness can, however, be tamed somewhat by placing a heavy load of camping gear in the canoe's bottom. The load will put more of the canoe in the water, making the canoe's bottom perform like a standard keel.

FLAT OR ROUND BOTTOM?

Virtually every text on wilderness canoeing recommends flat-bottom canoes over round-bottom ones, on the assumption that round-bottom hulls lack stability. Yet the fact remains that accomplished canoeists prefer round- or vee-bottom canoes for use on *every* type of water, from placid lakes to thundering rapids.

As far as stability is concerned, when it is loaded a round-bottom canoe feels nearly as stable as a flat-bottom one, and in reality the round hull is far more stable in rough water because you can control the canoe with your body. The responsiveness of the round hull permits you to make small balance adjustments easily. You can ride the waves and rapids and feel every movement of the canoe—like a jockey on a well-trained racehorse. Should you broach (turn broadside to the waves), you can immediately transfer your weight to expose more of the side of the canoe to the oncoming waves. The sluggishness of a flat-bottom canoe, on the other hand, prevents much real control except for steering.

Because of their curved shape, round bottoms are stronger than flat bottoms. Thus, round-bottom canoes do not usually require the additional reinforcement of keels. Keelless, flat-bottom canoes commonly suffer from lack of hull rigidity and have difficulty retaining their bottom shape when paddled through the water.

Additionally, round-bottom hulls are considerably faster than flat-bottom ones. Although you may not be concerned with speed, the time may come when you will need to paddle many miles against the wind on a large lake. At this time you will be grateful for whatever speed your canoe possesses.

Perhaps the biggest objection to round-bottom canoes is their lack of carrying capacity when compared to flat-bottom craft of the same length. This was a valid objection several decades ago, when most round-hulled canoes were narrow, shallow models with racing pedigrees. Today, however, there are many large, round-bottom canoes available—at reasonable prices. If carrying capacity is a problem, merely choose a bigger canoe.

SELECTING A STORE-BOUGHT CANOE

Since you usually can't take a new canoe out and try it before you buy, here are some things to look for and some tests to perform right in the store.

1. Use a tape measure to determine length, width, and depth. Don't believe the manufacturer's specifications. Is the canoe big enough for rough water?

2. Place the canoe on grass, a carpet, or the showroom floor. Climb in. Can you kneel beneath each seat? This is very important because kneeling increases stability, and you will often find it necessary to kneel in the rough water of rapids.

3. Manufacturers' listed canoe weights are almost always five to fifteen percent overoptimistic (I have never owned a canoe which weighed *less* than its advertised weight). Even identical canoe models from the same manufacturer vary in weight, sometimes by as much as eight pounds. (Aluminum canoes are an exception. Their weight is nearly identical to that advertised by the manufacturer.) Take a bathroom scale with you when you go canoe-shopping.

4. Climb out of the canoe and spin it around on the ground. If the canoe spins easily and is a keelless model, it probably has a fair amount of rocker. You can also look at the hull at ground level to see how much dead rise there is at the ends; there should be some. But the spin test is best. Even a keeled canoe will spin somewhat if there is sufficient rocker.

(It is important to realize that the spin test provides only a very rough estimate of a canoe's turning ability. To use this test effectively you should try several canoe models and compare them). Where possible, choose a keelless canoe with a fairly straight bottom line. You want some rocker, but not too much.

5. You will probably carry a wilderness canoe almost as much as you will paddle it. The carrying yoke or center thwart should be installed almost at the exact center of the canoe. Have the salesperson help you place the canoe on your shoulders (just let the center thwart rest on your neck). Is the canoe balanced, or is one end much heavier than the other? If the canoe is out of balance, can the center thwart be easily moved?

6. A wilderness canoe must be equipped with *painters,* or end lines. Ideally, the attachment point for these lines (the towing link) should be located as close to the water line as possible. Where lines are secured to the deck of a canoe, the force of the water acting on the canoe is so distant from the point of attachment of the painters that a quick pull of a rope can, in some rapids or currents, overturn the canoe. I nearly lost my life once when a canoe in which I was paddling upset while being lined down a difficult rapid. I made two errors which I will never repeat: lining a canoe with a person in it (me), and tying a rope to the deck plate, which is much too high.

7. Gunwales should be aluminum or wood so that holes can be drilled or brackets attached to function as *tie points* for ropes. In rough water you will want to secure your gear in the canoe, and it is nice to have attachment points along the gunwales. Some kinds of plastic crack under stress and don't stand up to extreme temperature changes.

8. Canoes built of nonbuoyant materials must have built-in flotation. Usually this consists of styrofoam blocks placed in sealed compartments at each end of the canoe. Make sure flotation does not interfere with front legroom.

9. To prevent bottom wobble, flat-bottom canoes should have an inner or outer keel, or they should have their bottoms reinforced with additional material.

As you look around for the ideal wilderness canoe, remember that most novice canoeists buy small, short canoes because they are light and easy to handle and store. As a result, many manufacturers design their small canoes for an inexperienced market, with high bows and sterns, plastic gunwales, flotation under the seats, big keels, and so on. Experienced canoeists usually select the longest and deepest canoes they can carry; hence, big canoes are usually designed to meet the needs of more knowledgeable paddlers. Most canoes 18 to 18½ feet long will meet many of the wilderness design requirements. This is not to say that shorter canoes have no place in the wilderness. There are some very suitable 16- and 17-foot models available—but you will have to know where to look for them.

THE CASE FOR THE SHORT CANOE

If your canoeing will be limited to the near wilderness of small streams and rivers, especially in areas where there is no real white water, a small, light canoe may be right for you. If you plan to do a lot of rock-dodging in shallow rapids or to twist your way down narrow, mountain-fed streams like the ones in North Carolina, Vermont, and West Virginia, a 16-foot deep-hulled canoe would be a good choice. Short canoes generally turn quickly and are light and easy to handle on portages.

Carrying long canoes through brushy areas, between trees, and up and down steep banks can be very frustrating. It is in these areas that the short canoe excels. And if you prefer to paddle alone, you will find a lightly loaded, narrow, 16-foot canoe to be fast, responsive, and easily maneuvered.

Canoes shorter than 16 feet, however, respond sluggishly to the paddle and have poor directional stability. With the exception of specialized white-water craft, such canoes are better adapted to portaging than paddling. There is little sense in buying, paddling, or carrying more canoe than you need. However, to attempt a rough-water wilderness voyage with a canoe that is too small is to invite disaster.

NEW CANOE DESIGNS

One of the most exciting improvements in canoe design has been the appearance of the asymmetric hull. Basically this consists of a long, narrow, somewhat flared bow with a fairly uniform taper and a fat, buoyant stern. The stern is made fuller than the bow (below the water line) because when a canoe is paddled through water it tends to create turbulence (a wake) at its tail end. The foamy nature of this turbulent

FIGURE 3. An asymmetric canoe in white-water competition. Canoe is an 18-foot 6-inch Sawyer Charger. (*Photo courtesy Sawyer Canoe Co.*)

water reduces the buoyancy of the canoe at the stern. The faster the craft is paddled, the less the buoyancy of the stern. At a speed of about six miles per hour the stern sinks sufficiently to make it appear that the canoe is being paddled uphill. To correct for this the stern is built wider (more buoyant) than the bow. The resulting canoe is easier to paddle, hence faster than conventionally designed craft (especially in water which is less than two or three feet deep).

Asymmetric canoes which are large enough for wilderness cruising are currently manufactured by Sawyer, Lincoln, and Moore (see Appendix C for complete listing of U.S. and Canada canoe makers). These super canoes are enlarged and slightly modified versions of smaller, flat-water racing craft. All are 18½ feet long and most are 14 to 15 inches deep with 32- to 36-inch beams. None have keels, and the majority have sufficient rocker to permit acceptably quick turns in fast water. Since these canoes were originally designed for white-water racing, they perform beautifully in heavy rapids and running waves. At present all are constructed of fiberglass or Kevlar (see Building Materials section).

In the hands of experienced crews, the super canoes are ideal for extended wilderness trips. Being experts' canoes, they require some finesse, as they are very tippy. When they are loaded, however, they feel quite stable and are fine for any kind of family canoeing. A recent trip down Minnesota's St. Croix River saw my asymmetric Sawyer Charger loaded with three adults, two kids, a cooler, picnic lunch, charcoal, and grill. And I had at least ten inches of freeboard. Unfortunately, these big canoes are expensive. At this writing prices begin around four hundred dollars. If you can afford one, it is well worth the money.

FREEBOARD

Even if you never take a far northern or arctic trip, you will be happiest with a big canoe, because it has adequate freeboard to weather out rough water. Some of the most popular canoe areas, like the Quetico-Superior wilderness of Minnesota-Canada and the Allagash wilderness waterway of Maine, are now so heavily traveled that finding unoccupied campsites has become a problem. The dense foliage and/or rocky nature of these areas prevents camping just anywhere, and camping areas are restricted for environmental reasons. I have been caught in a big *Norwester* (fierce wind out of the northwest) on an overpopulated lake more than once, with no suitable landing place in sight. At such times I was grateful for every inch of freeboard my canoe possessed.

I'll never forget the first day I paddled Yellowstone Lake in Yellowstone National Park, Wyoming. A strange combination of sea and mountain breezes suddenly caused the lake to turn on edge in midafternoon. What began as a pleasant morning paddle on quiet water finished as a mad dash to shore in 4-foot rollers. My 18-foot aluminum canoe barely made it to shore without swamping. (Since these conditions occur almost daily on Yellowstone Lake, canoeists should paddle in the early morning hours and camp by one or two P.M.)

While some experts recommend a minimum of 6 inches of free-board, no serious canoeist I know would think of using any canoe so heavily loaded on any but a mirror-calm lake. My own preference is a 9-inch minimum. A deep-hulled 18-foot canoe will easily ride that high if moderately loaded.

WEIGHT

Most people can comfortably carry canoes weighing up to seventy-five pounds. Beyond this weight canoes seem to get very heavy very fast. I know of few individuals who can tolerate more than eighty-five pounds for any great distance. There are a few big men who take pride in carrying heavy canoes. Some people select them because they are tougher than similar lightweight models. Whether the extra strength of a heavy canoe will save it from a pounding in heavy rapids is debatable, but one thing is evident—you will certainly be reluctant to carry a heavy canoe very far. In fact, many lightweight canoes have successfully negotiated wilderness waterways. I am slight of build and weigh only 135 pounds, and I can carry up to seventy-five pounds for about half a mile without stopping. If the weight increases or the distance is longer, my frame simply mashes down and refuses to move; hence I favor a lightweight canoe. Just as a good hunter can use a smaller caliber rifle because he is proficient in placing the shot, so, too, can an accomplished canoeist get by with a lighter weight canoe. There are limits, of course. No wilderness canoe can be fragile (although the birch-bark models certainly were), but it doesn't have to be built like a tank, either. Proficient canoeists seldom hit rocks directly or at high speeds. Their biggest problem in rough-water canoeing is usually swamping in heavy rapids. Under such conditions even a strong, well-built canoe can be broken in half or wrapped around a rock like a pretzel. Where the choice lies between a light, big canoe, and a heavy, strong, smaller model, choose the big canoe. It is important that you select a canoe that you can carry. Portaging in the wilderness is the rule, not the exception.

BUILDING MATERIALS

ALUMINUM

Aluminum canoes have achieved great popularity—and for good reason. They are inexpensive, incredibly tough, and virtually maintenance-free. Nearly all the canoes used by professional outfitters are aluminum, and except for the far north, where wood-canvas construction is still popular, nearly every serious wilderness tripper uses canoes built of this material.

Some manufacturers build lightweight aluminum canoes. The weight difference is in the thickness of the metal skin. Standard-weight models run around .050 inches thick, and the lightweights about .035 inches. Avoid the thin-skinned model if you will be using your canoe exclusively for shallow, rocky rivers—it won't hold up. Eighteen-foot aluminum canoes weigh about 85 to 90 pounds in standard weight and 67 to 72 pounds in light weight. The heavier canoe is considerably tougher, and if you can carry it, it is the best choice as it will deliver better service for more years. If you can't carry an 85-pound canoe, then you have no choice but to become a more proficient paddler and use extra care in handling your light canoe.

Since the machinery which produces aluminum canoes is very expensive, there have been few design innovations. Most aluminum-canoe designs are several years old; some date back to the 1940s. Few are very good. Almost invariably, 18-foot models are better designed than 17-footers, which still suffer from high, curved bows and sterns. At least two manufacturers (Grumman and Alumacraft) produce excellent 18½ foot canoes for serious wilderness tripping.

In buying an aluminum canoe, look for closely spaced, flush rivets. This is a sign of a properly tempered hull and is indicative of quality construction. Despite manufacturers' claims that spot welding is as strong as riveting, welded canoes seem to suffer greater damage on rocky white-water streams. A canoe which pulls its rivets in rough water can usually be repaired to its former strength by inserting oversize rivets. This repair can often be completed in the field with a minimum of tools and time. When spot welds separate, however, you must return the canoe to the factory to effect an acceptable repair. In essence, canoes with riveted hulls and fittings can be repaired by almost anybody; welded canoes cannot!

Almost any aluminum canoe seventeen feet or more long is suitable for wilderness tripping, as the flared ends, flat bottoms, and high sides make for great carrying capacity. (There are so many design factors which affect the determination of carrying capacity that manufacturers' recommendations are generally unreliable. The *real* carrying capacity of a canoe is almost always considerably less than that advertised.) Be-

FIGURE 4. Aluminum canoes are ideal for touring with young children who refuse to stay put for very long. (*Photo courtesy Grumman Co.*)

cause of their stability, aluminum canoes are ideal for touring with young children who refuse to stay put for very long.

For all its advantages, aluminum has a few drawbacks, the greatest of which is its tendency to cling to subsurface rocks. If an aluminum canoe strikes a rock below the water line, it will often be stopped completely. You may have no recourse but to get out of the canoe and push off the rock. The problem of sticking can be somewhat reduced by applying a good coat of paste wax to the bottom of the hull. For best results apply at least two coats of wax and buff each to silky smoothness. This is much less of a problem with canoes built of other materials.

Aluminum also dents, and try as you may, you will never remove the dents completely. Old aluminum canoes gradually take on the appearance of a high school shop ballpeen hammer project as they acquire dent upon dent.

FIBERGLASS REINFORCED PLASTIC

Two decades ago it was nearly impossible to find a properly designed fiberglass canoe that was sufficiently strong and light for extended wilderness touring. Now, however, there are a variety of suitable models available. Unfortunately, prices tend to be high—sometimes hundreds of dollars more than for the equivalent size of aluminum models.

Most big fiberglass canoes were designed by canoe enthusiasts for canoe enthusiasts. Those built by Chicagoland Canoe Base, Lincoln, Mad River, Moore, Sawyer, and Old Town represent some of the finest rough-water designs currently in production, and are certainly worth the money if you want a superb paddling canoe that is exceptionally beautiful, very tough, and acceptably light. Small fiberglass canoes are also available at much lower prices, but nearly all lack the necessary freeboard to negotiate the heavy rapids and waves encountered on a wilderness canoe trip.

Where use will be limited to lazy, picturesque streams and creeks like many in Iowa, Indiana, and Missouri, small fiberglass canoes are ideal, for they are very light and paddle effortlessly. But for extended touring under a variety of conditions, think more than twice before you buy a fiberglass model smaller than 18 feet long, 13½ inches deep, and 34 inches wide.

In buying a fiberglass canoe, make sure you specify *hand lay-up;* this means that the glass cloth is laid into the mold by hand. Some inexpensive canoes are made with chopped glass that is sprayed into place, which often results in lack of uniformity in hull thickness. Hand lay-up is stronger, lighter, and . . . much more expensive. You can tell hand lay-up at a glance, as you can see the outline of the glass weave in the inside of the hull.

ABS (ACRYLONITRILE BUTADIENE STYRENE)

Conventionally constructed canoes built of ABS plastic have achieved only limited success, in spite of the fact that they compare favorably in weight with aluminum models of similar size. Commercial outfitters who tried conventional ABS canoes have generally been dissatisfied. They found that these canoes just don't hold up as well as aluminum craft. Additionally, ABS plastic canoes are not cheap, and, to date, well-designed models suitable for extended wilderness tripping are not available.

However, when expanded to a foam (Royalex, made by Uniroyal), ABS is an exceptional canoe-building material. Royalex differs from ordinary ABS plastic in that it is laminated and vacuum-formed under intense heat and pressure so that many tiny air pockets exist. The resulting product, called a *thermoplastic laminate,* is very strong, lightweight, and naturally buoyant. Unlike fiberglass, Royalex seldom breaks; rather, it dents, and dents can be removed with a hot iron (with some effort). Although Royalex canoes have been available for more than a decade, they have not achieved much popularity, mostly due to the high cost of vacuum-molding the plastic material.

Nevertheless, foam ABS is perhaps the toughest material yet devised for canoes. Canoes built of Royalex are nearly impossible to puncture, and they "snick" over subsurface rocks so easily that even a mediocre canoeist has little difficulty making it through a twisting "rock garden" —while paddlers of aluminum canoes are still pushing off rocks, Royalex owners are hundreds of feet downstream. Unfortunately, unless the bottom of a Royalex canoe is reinforced with extra layers of material or is well rounded, it will have a tendency to ripple or "oil-can" in rough water. Long-distance racers are very finicky about oil-canning, and hence don't like Royalex. Racers do everything possible to stiffen the bottoms of their canoes to make them faster.

Although canoes built of fiberglass, wood, and wood and canvas are often faster, Royalex models have enjoyed much success in rocky white-

FIGURE 5. A ROYALEX canoe on Section IV of the infamous Chatooga River (where the movie *Deliverance* was filmed). The paddler is Dave Shupe of Crossville, Tennessee; the canoe is a 16-foot Blue Hole. The paddle is also made by the Blue Hole Company. (*Photo courtesy of Blue Hole Canoe Co.*)

water races, mainly due to their ability to wobble over rocks. Once you
get over your initial fear of the jellylike bottom, the fact that ABS
canoes are almost indestructible and as maintenance-free as aluminum
will probably attract you to them.

KEVLAR 49

Kevlar hit the market commercially in 1972. The fabric looks much
like fiberglass cloth, only its properties (and price) are much different.
Kevlar 49 composites have a tensile strength about forty percent higher
than epoxy-fiberglass and a specific gravity of 1.45 grams per cubic
centimeter, versus 2.55 for glass. This means that canoes built of Kevlar
are much stronger and lighter than equivalent glass models. Additionally,
the impact, tear, and penetration resistance of Kevlar is much superior to
glass. Because of the great expense of the material, nearly all Kevlar
boats are well designed. Kevlar canoes typically run $150 to $250 more
than identical glass models.

According to extensive tests performed by Dupont, some types of
construction have resulted in a 33 percent weight savings over comparable glass canoes, plus a high level of durability and damage tolerance.
In conventional construction, by using Kevlar five to ten pounds can
easily be cut from a seventy-five-pound canoe while *adding* rigidity and
durability. Like Royalex, Kevlar has a great deal of flex, which is dis-
concerting until you get used to it. The flex can be eliminated by bracing
the hull with ribs, but this would add weight and reduce bottom
elasticity.

Although perhaps not as tough as Royalex, Kevlar shares with
fiberglass one important advantage—its ability to be laid into a mold by
hand. This hand lay-up means that it is easy to redesign an existing
canoe hull, or to attempt fresh new designs, without a large investment
in expensive dies or molds. For this reason, plus the high strength and
very light weight of the fabric, Kevlar-built canoes have achieved
enormous popularity among canoe enthusiasts in the few years they have
been available.

CEDAR STRIP CANOES—THE ONES THAT WIN RACES

Most of the canoes that win long-distance flat-water races are hand-
built of cedar or redwood strips, nailed to a form, glued together, and

FIGURE 6. A hand-built Wonacott cedar strip cruising canoe. Length—18 feet, depth—13 inches, width—36 inches, weight—65 pounds. (*Photo courtesy of Wonacott Canoes, Inc.*)

covered with fiberglass cloth and polyester or epoxy resin (the nails are removed prior to glassing). The result is a very beautiful, very light, and very fast canoe. Since construction is all done by hand, the few companies that produce this style canoe command high prices (eight hundred dollars and up). Strip canoes, however, are easily built by anyone with power tools, basic woodworking know-how, and patience! They are very inexpensive to make. Easy-to-follow plans for the construction of several excellent canoe models are available at low cost from the Minnesota Canoe Association, P.O. Box 14177, University Station, Minneapolis, Minnesota 55401; and the U.S. Canoe Association, RR #1, Box 644, Bristol, Indiana 46507.

It is interesting to note that the greatest cross-continent canoe safari of the twentieth century was completed in a canoe built of Sitka spruce strips and fiberglass. In April 1971 Verlen Kruger of DeWitt, Michigan, and Clint Waddell of Saint Paul, Minnesota, launched a hand-built twenty-one-foot strip canoe at Montreal's Lachine docks on the Saint Lawrence River. The two men paddled 6500 miles across some of the roughest waterways in North America, and terminated their trip at the Bering Sea in Alaska just five months later. Vital canoe statistics were:

LENGTH : 21 feet
WIDTH MEASURED 3 INCHES OFF THE BOTTOM : 27 inches; AT THE CENTER
    THWART : 34 inches
DEPTH : 18 inches at the bow; 12½ inches rest of length
WEIGHT : 85 pounds
SEATS : Sawyer molded fiberglass, bucket-type
YOKES : Form-fitted center yoke for one-man carry, and a pad and yoke
    at each end for two-man carry
COVER : 8-ounce waterproof nylon snap-on for complete protection from
    spray

Experienced paddlers will recognize Kruger's hand-built canoe as a lengthened version of the standard Canadian racer. The Waddell-Kruger expedition to the Bering Sea is the most fantastic canoe voyage of our time—perhaps of any time. The fact that this trip was safely completed in a modern canoe of revolutionary design should do much to dispel the myth that canoes have changed little since the time of the Indian birch barks.

WOOD-CANVAS CANOES

The return-to-nature movement has brought an increased demand for wood-canvas canoes. In fact, Canada's Chestnut Canoe Company, which is the world's largest manufacturer of these traditional craft, reports that sales have been rising steadily by 25 to 30 percent a year—and prices have been going up accordingly. The average Chestnut canoe now costs well over four hundred dollars, and the least expensive, American-made Old Town runs twice that amount. Nevertheless, even at these high prices a wood-canvas canoe is a bargain. A typical eighteen-foot canoe, for example, requires over eighty board feet of high-grade lumber (most of it white cedar) and more than three hundred solid brass tacks.

Since there is a great deal of hand work involved in the production of canvas-covered canoes, models can be altered at the factory to suit your tastes. You can specify extra depth, lighter weight, heavier or lighter grade canvas, and so on. This, in addition to the sixty-one different models already produced by Chestnut, makes the range of sizes and designs offered by this company almost unlimited.

In the United States the largest and best-known maker of wood-

FIGURE 7. Old Town wood-canvas canoes on the Eastmain River in Quebec. Note the rigid tote boxes used to protect breakables. (*Photo courtesy of Old Town Canoe Co.*)

canvas canoes is Old Town. Because of the high cost of labor and materials, Old Town models are extremely expensive. The canoes are superbly constructed, however, and reflect an uncompromised standard of quality. Additionally, the purchase of an Old Town canoe is an investment, for these craft depreciate little (on the contrary, they often appreciate).

Wood-canvas canoes are much tougher than most people think. They have quite a lot of flex in their hulls, and like fiberglass and Royalex canoes, they slide over rocks easily. When they are new they weigh about the same as equivalent size standard-weight aluminum models, but after they've been on the trail for some time they begin to absorb water; overall weight can increase by ten percent or more.

If you are strong enough to carry a water-soaked canoe of wood and cloth, and you can afford one, the annual chore of patching, sanding, and painting will be more than made up for by the joys of ownership.

THE TOUGHNESS MYTH

Regardless of the material a canoe is built of, manufacturers will tell you that their canoes are the toughest afloat. Fiberglass canoe builders take pride in reporting how many times stronger than aluminum their canoe models are. Consider this: many of the synthetics may take more abuse in direct impact than heavy, heat-treated aluminum, but they are subject to considerably more damage from abrasion. If you will be grinding your canoe against rocks, dragging it over sand bars, or treating it in other abusive ways, then get an aluminum canoe. It will outlast several other canoes of different materials. However, if you baby your canoe in areas where abrasion is a problem, you may get better service, performance, and enjoyment from a nonaluminum canoe.

ON BUYING A USED CANOE

Now that you are familiar with canoe design and construction, you should have a pretty good idea of what you want in a canoe. The following guidelines will help you get the best deal on a good used canoe:

1. Know the retail value of the canoe *before* you talk to the owner. Figure on paying up to eighty percent of the current retail price for well-cared-for, top-line aluminum canoes, and around fifty percent for

lesser known aluminum, fiberglass, and ABS cheapies. Quality-built fiberglass, Kevlar, and Royalex canoes generally command sixty to seventy-five percent of their new retail cost, if they have been well kept.

2. If you are trying to save money, purchase a canoe with a hole in it. Contrary to popular belief, canoes are easily patched (see Chapter 7— Salvage and Repair). Check with commercial outfitters, who often sell damaged canoes cheaply (shoddy equipment is bad for their image). With ingenuity and the proper repair materials, you can often restore a canoe to nearly new condition.

3. If you select a used fiberglass canoe, choose one with adequate size and depth. Fiberglass canoes will generally ride about two to four inches lower in the water than aluminum models of the same size, so their carrying capacity will be reduced.

4. Turn used canoes upside down and sight along the keel. Don't buy a canoe with a "hogged" (bent-in) keel. Once a keel is bent, it is almost impossible to straighten it properly.

5. Carefully sight along each gunwale. It is very difficult to straighten heat-treated aluminum gunwales, although a hammer and piece of two-by-four can be used to improve aesthetics somewhat. Plastic and wood gunwales which are cracked or broken must be completely replaced.

6. On aluminum canoes, check for stressed or pulled rivets which could cause leakage.

7. Check fiberglass canoes for signs of hull delamination. Home-built and factory prefabricated kit models especially should be carefully examined, as the quality of these canoes depends entirely upon the skill of the builder. This doesn't mean that hand-built canoes are bad. On the contrary, many canoe clubs own their own molds, and club members produce superb canoes at a fraction of the cost (and weight) of factory-built models. A well constructed club-built canoe may be an excellent investment. Occasionally a racing enthusiast will offer a nearly new canoe for sale at little more than the original cost of the building materials, simply because he or she is displeased with the canoe's performance. Canoe clubs and canoe races are good places to frequent if you are looking for a good, inexpensive canoe.

In summary, select a canoe of adequate size, with sufficient depth beneath the seats to permit kneeling. Be certain that the keel line of the canoe is not bent, and check for damaged fittings. Eliminate from consideration any fiberglass or Kevlar canoe which shows signs of hull delamination, and be knowledgeable of the canoe's value before you buy. Lastly, join a canoe club. Club membership will bring you into contact with skilled paddlers and canoe builders and will increase your chances of locating a good used canoe at a reasonable price.

3.
Tuning the Canoe for Better Performance

Most new canoes require some "tuning" to deliver optimum performance on wilderness waterways. Here are some ways to make your craft safer and more enjoyable to paddle and carry.

CARRYING YOKE

Canoes are usually carried by one person, with the aid of a padded carrying yoke (an extra-cost item). Aluminum yokes are channeled to fit over the existing center thwart (an exception is the excellent Alumacraft yoke, which is supplied as standard equipment in lieu of a center thwart), while wooden yokes replace the thwart completely. Most manufacturers install the center thwart or yoke in a location determined by a formula, which is often subject to some error. For example, the yoke on one of my canoes was misplaced by four inches, making the craft so tail-heavy that it was impossible to carry.

The most satisfactory method of balancing a canoe is to try it on

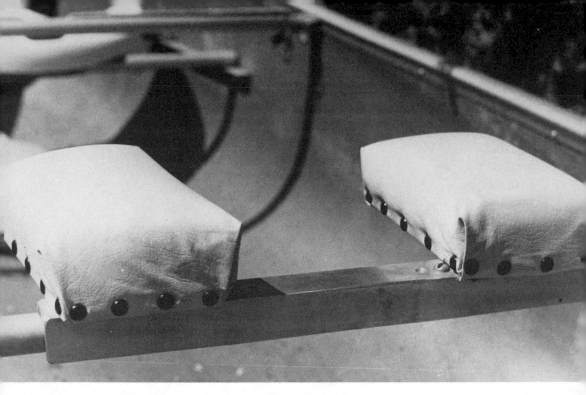

FIGURE 8a. Aluminum yokes are channeled to fit over the existing center thwart. (*Sawyer Canoe Company yoke*)

FIGURE 8b. The excellent Alumacraft yoke is supplied as standard equipment in lieu of a center thwart.

your shoulders. I like just enough weight in the tail so that the bow will rise very slowly when the canoe is shouldered. I consider a canoe out of balance if more than gentle pressure is required to bring it back to a horizontal position. A friend of mine, on the other hand, likes his canoe perfectly balanced, as he prefers to walk with his hands in his pockets. You can easily change the balance on your canoe by reinstalling the yoke in a new set of mounting holes drilled in the gunwales.

If you are very broad-shouldered you will like the spacing of factory-made yoke pads, but if you're of average build you will need to move the pads closer together and to change their angle somewhat. Most people prefer pads mounted at right angles to the yoke bar, with a distance of 6½ to 7 inches between them.

If you do much portaging you will want a wooden yoke. The springiness and warmth of wood against your neck makes for more comfort than the inflexibility and coldness of aluminum. Make your yoke from ash, oak, or maple, and finish to a ⅝ inch thickness (figure 9). Completed width should be 2 to 2½ inches to assure adequate strength. Cut two 8-by-3½ inch yoke pad blocks from ⅜ inch plywood, and pile 6

FIGURE 8c. If you do much portaging you will want a wooden yoke. The springiness and warmth of wood against your neck makes for more comfort than the inflexibility and coldness of aluminum. (The yoke in the photo is hand-built.)

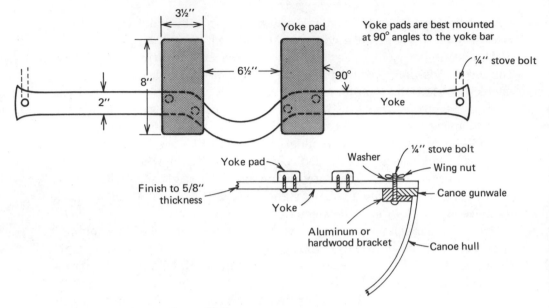

FIGURE 9. *Making a Canoe Yoke*
Note: Yoke is mounted on *top* of gunwales, not under them.

inches of polyurethane foam on each block (use pillow padding available at any discount store). Compress each pad to about 2½ inches and cover with a light-colored naugahide to reflect heat (I found the difference in surface temperature between a black and a white pad in strong sunlight to be 35 degrees!). Staple naugahide into place and finish with upholstery tacks. I have found it best to secure wood yokes to gunwales with a simple clamp device and wing nuts. Screwing them to gunwales looks nice, but the flex of the yoke can cause splits to develop near the screws.

SHOCK CORDS AND RUBBER ROPES

On a recent trip down the flooded Groundhog River in northern Ontario, my partner and I inadvertently ran a five-foot falls. When the bow of our eighteen-foot aluminum canoe punched through the big roller below, the canoe filled with several inches of water. We spun broadside in the rapids swamping completely. Fortunately, our four watertight Duluth packs stayed put throughout the run, providing us with sufficient buoyancy to keep afloat. We retained enough freeboard to paddle cautiously ashore.

In white water you need the additional flotation provided by watertight packs, and you can only utilize this flotation if packs are well secured in the canoe. If your canoe is aluminum, drill a series of holes, three-eights inch diameter, along the gunwales about four inches apart. These holes will provide anchor points for cords and steel hooks to which heavy-duty rubber ropes are attached. If the gunwales of your canoe have water-drain slots (as on wood-canvas models), you can hook your cords or rubber ropes directly to them. The solid rails of most fiberglass and ABS boats, however, present more of a problem. Usually it is possible to drill small holes through the inwale or just below the gunwale. Short loops of parachute cord can then be run through these holes to provide attachment points for your security ropes.

Run at least two rubber ropes across each pack, and where very heavy rapids will be encountered add a length of nylon parachute cord. Tie the cord with a quick release knot (see Chapter 9—Tying It All Together) so you won't have difficulty salvaging your gear if you overturn. You can stuff your bailing sponge, fishing gear, and loose articles under the ropes to prevent loss in an upset. The parachute cords will prevent *pack-bob* (packs rising up in a water-filled canoe). Rubber ropes permit quick removal and replacement of packs when making portages. It is a real pain in the neck to constantly tie and untie a network of ropes.

Drill holes in thwarts and deck plates and install lightweight, fabric-covered shock cord. Wet clothes and oddities placed under the corded thwarts will stay put in high winds and on portages. An especially good place for your map is under a shock-corded thwart. The loss of a map can be very serious on a wilderness trip, for, unlike backpacking, there are no trails to guide the way. A good friend of mine once traded a thirty-five-cent map for several dollars worth of fishing lures to a party who had lost theirs when they overturned in a set of rapids. You should carry an extra map on all wilderness trips, but the one in use should always be well secured in place.

PAINTERS

As previously stated, end lines or painters should be attached as close to the water line of a canoe as possible. A hole can usually be drilled below the deck plate and a hollow plastic tube epoxied into place. The tube will keep water from leaking into the canoe when the bow plunges in rapids. Make sure the plastic tube is of sufficient size to allow passage of a ¼ inch diameter painter. It is important that end lines be available when you need them; they should not be tied into place, and they should not be left hanging loose to entangle a swimmer in the event of an upset. Once on a northern Canadian trip a canoe got away while it was being unloaded in an eddy above a bouldery falls. When we retrieved it at the base of the falls, one deck plate had been torn off. A painter, which was attached to the deck plate and left lying loose in the canoe's bottom, had streamed out and caught between two rocks.

The best solution for keeping painters immediately available *and* out of the way is to coil and stuff them under a loop of shock cord attached to the deck. Thus stored, they can be released by a simple tug of the end. They will not stream out independently if you overturn, and will remain in place while portaging. Use bright-colored ¼ inch polypropylene rope for painters. Poly rope is very light and won't absorb water; you will be able to find it more easily should you capsize in foamy rapids. For serious wilderness trips I attach two lines to each end of the canoe—an 18-foot poly rope and a 50-foot nylon line. This gives me an instant choice between a short, nonsnagging rope and a long, tracking line. Where two ropes are attached to the same end of a canoe, each should be stored under its own shock cord to prevent tangling.

GRAB LOOPS

Attach a 6-inch-long poly rope to each end of your canoe. Should you swamp in rapids, you can quickly grab the loop, which may be more accessible than a painter. Grab loops are also convenient handholds for lifting the canoe.

GLARE REDUCTION

Glare from the deck plate of an aluminum canoe can be hazardous if you are in a set of rapids requiring complex maneuvering. An easy solution is to paint each deck plate flat black. The person in the bow will appreciate this small bit of forethought, and you will damage your canoe less, if the forward paddler can see better.

SPLASH COVERS

Whenever I show up at a white-water event with my seventeen-foot shoe-keeled aluminum canoe, I get condescending suggestions from kayakers regarding my paddling technique, the fragility of my canoe, and what to do when (not *if*) I wipe-out. The trouble with open canoes is that in heavy rapids they fill with water, making it impossible for even an Olympic paddler to control them. Kayaks and slalom canoes don't have this problem, since they are completely decked over.

After several years of continuous harassment, I decided to make my canoe invincible by covering it with waterproof nylon. Unfortunately I can't run a sewing machine well enough to make a canoe cover, and every commercial model I looked at cost several hundred dollars. I found that only a few companies offered splash covers, and these were designed for specific canoe models. I got an estimate from an upholstery shop once, but it was over two hundred dollars.

Fortunately I have a good friend who is a genius; his name is Paul Swanstrom. One day Paul strolled over, ran his hand along the deck of my aging Grumman, and exclaimed, "Heck, we can build a cover for under forty dollars and complete it in less than a day." Paul and I have done a fair amount of white-water rafting together, and after a good many raft repairs he became a great believer in glue (that's right, glue) to hold things together. "We'll glue the cover together and secure it to the canoe with a stainless steel cable," said Paul. "We can make a cable tightener similar to a front-throw cable-release ski binding out of scrap iron and aluminum tubing. The only sewing will be the spray skirts. The cable binding and quickie release will give us an on-off cover in sixty seconds."

Materials:

VINYL-COATED NYLON (any color): 8-ounce weight per square yard or heavier, and enough to cover the canoe. For a 17-foot canoe you need a piece of material 17 feet long by 40 inches wide. Don't get more than this; you don't need it. If you will use your cover only occasionally, you can use a fabric as light as 2.2 ounces per square yard. Lightweight covers, however, will not stand up to the heavy pounding of waves and abrasion of rocks. A heavier material will increase the weight of the cover by only a pound or two, but durability will be increased greatly.

BOSTIK ADHESIVE #4585: one quart (available from Bostik division, USM Corp., Middleton, Massachusetts 01949). It is extremely important that you use the right glue. Read the label *very* carefully before you accept a substitute for Bostik #4585, and before you begin test the adhesive on two pieces of scrap vinyl.

LARGE SYRINGE FOR INJECTING GLUE: the glue is too thick to brush on. It is applied to the vinyl in a narrow bead and spread out with a *plastic squeegee* (a must).

1/8″ DIAMETER STAINLESS-STEEL CABLE (get the most flexible possible): 38 feet for a 17-foot canoe (or substitute 1/4 inch diameter nylon rope).

24 STAINLESS STEEL OR ALUMINUM U-SHAPED FITTINGS: we looked all over to find a suitable fitting for mounting on the canoe hull. We finally settled on a soft-tempered, nickel-plated steel bracket which we bent to our requirements (see figure 10).

24 ALUMINUM RIVETS: for installing the U-shaped fittings.

2 FEET OF ONE-INCH SQUARE THICK-WALLED ALUMINUM CHANNEL: for making the front fitting.

12-INCH LENGTH OF 3/4 INCH DIAMETER ALUMINUM TUBING (thick-walled): for making the handle which attaches to the steel cable.

12 FEET OF HEAVY-DUTY FABRIC-COVERED SHOCK CORD: to be used in securing the spray skirts.

Preparation

The most difficult part of making the splash cover is the front fitting (cable-locking device). Paul's original model required a good deal of precision welding. It is possible to avoid manufacture of this fitting by substituting a pair of front-throw cable-release ski bindings. The ski bindings will need to be riveted to an aluminum or scrap iron backing plate before installing them on the canoe. The real advantage of the homemade unit over the commercial ski binding is its longer length of throw, which permits faster and easier installation and removal of the splash cover.

You can also substitute a simple screw-actuated tightener at each end of the steel cable; however, this will eliminate the quick on-off feature of the cover.

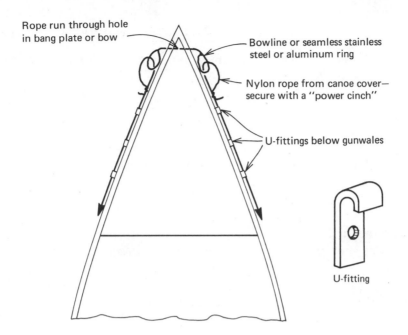

Rope run through hole
in bang plate or bow

Bowline or seamless stainless
steel or aluminum ring

Nylon rope from canoe cover—
secure with a "power cinch"

U-fittings below gunwales

U-fitting

FIGURE 10. *Using Nylon Rope and a Quick-Release Knot to Secure the Canoe Cover*

A still simpler solution is to substitute ¼ inch diameter nylon rope for the steel cable and a quick-release knot for the sophisticated cable release. To make a rope lock, run a short length of ¼ inch nylon line through the hole in the canoe's bang plate (or bow) and tie a bowline (see Chapter 9—Tying It All Together) at each end, or attach seamless aluminum or stainless steel rings to the rope (figure 10). Secure the nylon lines from the canoe cover to the bowlines or rings with a power-cinch (see Chapter 9) and quick-release knot. A major advantage of nylon rope over steel cable is that it permits the splash cover to be rolled compactly when not in use—an asset while portaging. On the negative side, rope-tightened covers, although adequate, are neither as secure nor as tight as those installed with steel cables.

If you decide to make the cable-locking device, proceed as follows: cut (use a saber saw) and bend a piece of aluminum channel about 17 inches long to the approximate shape illustrated in figure 11b. The channel should fit the contours of the canoe's bow tightly (figure 11a). Smooth all rough edges with a file and attach the unit to the canoe's bow with a pin and cotter key (figure 11a). Make the locking handle

for the unit out of aluminum tubing or channel as illustrated (figure
11b), and install the stainless-steel cable.

Procedure

Most commercial canoe covers are installed with a row of snaps
beneath the gunwales. Unfortunately even the best grade of coated material shrinks, and after a while the snaps won't fit. And if you ever upset
in a difficult rapid and your cover comes off and wraps around your
legs . . . need I say more? Flat-water racers install covers by snugging
a rope beneath the rather straight gunwales of their canoes. But this
isn't secure enough for white water. The splash cover described here is
easy and inexpensive to make, and is so securely attached to the canoe
that there is little, if any, possibility of it coming loose in a heavy rapid.

Begin manufacture of the cover by riveting U-shaped brackets, open
side down, all around the canoe about 16 inches apart, 2 inches below
the gunwales.

Lay out the fabric lengthwise across the top of the canoe, wrong
side out, and snug up the rope (cable) around it. Pull the material drum-
taut all around, then snap the cable (rope) into the U-brackets to lock
the fabric in place.

Cut the nylon so that it extends about 3 inches below the rope or
cable, and cut out holes for the U-fittings. Apply adhesive sparingly
above and below the cable, taking care not to get any on the cable. Allow
the glue to dry (about two minutes) and flip the fabric into place all the
way around. Bostik acts like a contact cement, so once the two pieces of
glued material touch you are stuck with a permanent bond. You can
insert the cable inside a plastic tube (with cutouts for the U-fittings)
to make it slide more easily during tightening if you prefer, but this will
increase the overall stuffed size of the cover.

Next, turn the cover right side out so the glued edges are hidden
and cut holes for the paddlers. Before you cut, make sure you locate the
holes properly. Make the holes large enough so that you can assume
either a kneeling or sitting position. (The nice thing about glue is that
it enables you to restructure the openings if you goof.)

Make your spray skirts out of the same material as the cover, or,
for greater comfort, use ultra-lightweight, plastic-coated nylon. Cut two
pieces of fabric 26 inches wide and make each piece 2 inches longer than

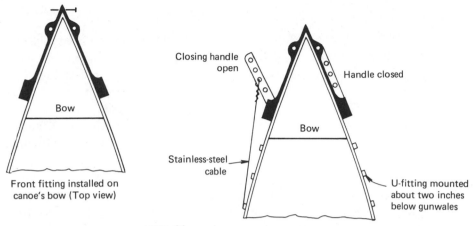

Closing handle open

Handle closed

Bow

Bow

Stainless-steel cable

U-fitting mounted about two inches below gunwales

Front fitting installed on canoe's bow (Top view)

FIGURE 11a.

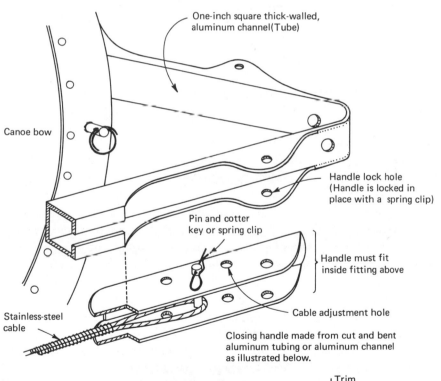

One-inch square thick-walled, aluminum channel(Tube)

Canoe bow

Handle lock hole (Handle is locked in place with a spring clip)

Pin and cotter key or spring clip

Handle must fit inside fitting above

Stainless-steel cable

Cable adjustment hole

Closing handle made from cut and bent aluminum tubing or aluminum channel as illustrated below.

Closing handle should be formed in one piece from flat stock, but may be riveted together using two pieces cut from a square tube as shown on the right.

Trim

Cut

a

b

a

b

Rivet

FIGURE 11b.

the circumference of the holes in the cover to allow an ample seam allowance. Glue or sew each piece of material to form a simple 26-inch-high cylinder and attach one end of each cylinder to a cover opening.

When you are satisfied with the location and attachment of your spray skirts, install heavyweight fabric-covered shock cord in each spray-skirt top and pucker the material around your waist. In a kayak or decked slalom canoe, the spray skirts are not permanently attached to the deck. In a spill the paddler pulls a cord that releases the skirt from the boat. Once the skirt is released, water enters the craft and the pressure equalizes, making it possible for the canoeist to climb out of the cockpit (the spray skirt remains attached to the wearer). In a fabric-covered canoe, however, the skirts are an integral part of the cover and there is a good deal of water pressure on them when you are upside down. I have found it best, therefore, to tie the shock cord in a simple bow around my waist. I can ordinarily exert enough power with my legs to push myself free of the cover if I capsize, but just in case I can't, a simple pull of the elastic cord will cause the skirt to spring open and release me.

More than casual attention should be paid to spray-skirt escape. In securing the spray-skirt to your waist, *do not, under any conditions, substitute rope for shock-cord*—it may make escape from your cover impossible.

Although you will be considerably safer in heavy rapids and waves with a covered canoe, you will have to be very careful that you don't let your cover cloud your good judgment. Canoeists who paddle covered boats have a tendency to get very bold—they think they can run anything. When you are paddling with an experienced white-water group and are properly clothed in a life jacket, wet suit, and helmet, you can afford to take a few chances; in the wilderness you can't. Northern rivers run very cold, and should you capsize in one you will be able to remain in the water for only a few minutes. Your boots and heavy clothing will make swimming difficult. Even with a life jacket you will be lucky to survive. For this reason some very experienced wilderness canoeists prefer to travel without covers, or, at best, with a simple half-cover which extends from the bow deck to the front thwart.

For those who would paddle the rapid-filled waters of the northwest and Canadian arctic, the advantages of a splash cover are apparent. Traditional kayak routes on rivers like the Snake and Salmon (Idaho's infamous "river of no return") are fair game for your covered canoe. However, unlike a decked kayak, a fabric-covered canoe is too stable to be "eskimo-rolled" upright once it is upside down. An upset in dangerous waters may mean a long and difficult swim; consider the consequences if your bravery exceeds your ability.

4.
Portaging the Canoe

Whether you paddle the great rivers of the far north or the peaceful lakes and streams of the near wilderness, you will encounter impassable rapids, waterfalls, or other obstacles which will make it necessary for you to carry your canoe and equipment over land. After many hours afloat in a cramped canoe, a portage is usually a welcome change of pace. Portage trails give you a chance to stretch your legs, exercise your muscles, and become reattuned to the sights and sounds of the forest.

Although canoes, equipment, and paddling methods have changed considerably during the past century, the techniques of portaging has remained the same. I say *technique* because portaging is as much an art as a feat of physical strength. I have seen ninety-pound girls lift seventy-five-pound canoes single-handed and carry them nonstop over very rough trails for more than a quarter of a mile. And I have known two hundred-pound men who could not carry the same canoe more than two hundred feet without dropping it on the nearest boulder. A canoe on land is out of its native habitat, and in the hands of a thoughtless or careless person may suffer great damage.

Outfitters in the Quetico-Superior wilderness of Minnesota seldom get more than six years of satisfactory service out of their rental canoes. They report that their canoes suffer much greater damage due to careless handling on land than from striking obstacles in the water. Consequently, many youth camps have initiated the "wet-foot" policy. This means that canoes must be loaded, unloaded, picked up, and set down in a minimum of twelve inches of water. Since wet-footing eliminates virtually all land injuries, organizations practicing this method often boast more than twenty years of good service from their canoes (for example, the Charles Sommers Scout Canoe Base, in Ely, Minnesota, maintains a fleet of very old, nearly dent-free, aluminum canoes).

I am not an advocate of the wet-foot policy. Spending several hours a day with wet, shriveled-up feet is not my idea of a good time. With care it is perfectly possible to stand on land, or in an inch or two of water, and load and unload even a very fragile canoe without damaging it. Virtually all land damage occurs while picking a canoe up or setting it down. For this reason a thorough understanding of lift-and-carry techniques is essential to a dent- and gouge-free canoe trip.

ONE-PERSON LIFT-AND-CARRY

On wilderness trips I seldom pick up a canoe by myself. It just takes too much effort, and I would rather save my energy for the portage trail. There will, however, be many times when you will need to lift a canoe to your shoulders alone, so you should become proficient in the one-person lift-and-carry.

PROCEDURE

If you are right-handed, stand at the center left side of the canoe, facing it. Pull the canoe up by the near gunwale and grasp the center of the yoke with your right hand (figure 12a). Keeping your legs well apart, flip the canoe onto your thighs with a quick pull of the right arm. As the canoe comes up, grab the far gunwale with your left hand just forward of the yoke (the canoe should now be almost wholly supported by your thighs). Next, transfer your right hand to a position just back of the yoke on the gunwale (figure 12b). Thus your left hand is forward of the yoke on the top gunwale, and your right hand is just behind it on the bottom gunwale.

FIGURE 12a. *One-person lift*. Step 1. *Right* hand grasps yoke center and canoe is spun to thighs.

FIGURE 12b. Step 2. *Left* hand grasps top gunwale forward of yoke and canoe is balanced on thighs.

FIGURE 12c. Step 3. With a quick upward push from your right knee, snap the canoe up and around, over your head.

FIGURE 12d. Settle the yoke pads on your shoulders and . . . *relax!*

The next part is the hardest. With a quick upward push from your right knee, snap the canoe up and around, over your head (figure 12c), and settle the yoke pads on your shoulders (figure 12d). Many beginners have difficulty here because they are fearful of getting their necks twisted up in the yoke. In reality, this almost never occurs. It's sort of like closing both eyes and touching your nose with a fist. Just as you always seem to successfully locate your nose, so too will you always find the portage yoke when the canoe comes up. The key to lifting the canoe is determination and a quick snap. You would have to be very strong to pick up even a light canoe slowly, whereas a person of small stature will have little difficulty raising canoes weighing up to ninety pounds if he or she is snappy about it. Although the one-person lift requires some practice to perfect, it is important to learn it properly, for there are many times when you will need to use this skill. When teaching this lift to new canoeists, I often tell them to remember the words *right, left, right* to insure that their hands will be properly positioned during the pick-up sequence. Thus:

1. *Right* hand grasps yoke center and canoe is spun to thighs.
2. *Left* hand grasps top gunwale forward of yoke.
3. *Right* hand grasps lower gunwale just back of yoke and canoe is snapped to shoulders.

Beginners often have trouble carrying the canoe once they have it in position. The key to carrying a canoe is not strength at all; rather, it is learning to relax under the portage yoke. In order to accomplish this successfully, it is best that you have one or two friends help you position the canoe on your shoulders. When the yoke pads settle into place, stand perfectly straight and reach forward with your hands to grasp the gunwales. Place your fingers on the shelflike lip of the gunwales and your thumbs on the opposite side. If the canoe is properly balanced (slightly tail-heavy), light pressure from your fingers will bring the bow down to a horizontal position. The canoe is now ready for portaging. To get used to the yoke, stand in place and drop your left arm to your side. Most of the canoe's weight will now rest on your right shoulder. Repeat, dropping the other arm. You will become less tired on portages if you continually change the weight from shoulder to shoulder. When you feel confident under the yoke, you are ready for your first short hike. Walk about two hundred feet and set the canoe down. Rest up a while and try again—only this time go twice as far. If you feel good after this second session, you probably have the mechanics down pat. Your shoulder muscles may hurt somewhat, but if you feel a stabbing pain the canoe is not properly positioned. Most likely you are hunching in fear under the yoke instead of standing straight. Several short practice sessions will teach you the technique of portaging much better than further discussion.

TWO- OR THREE-PERSON LIFT, ONE-PERSON CARRY

Even if you are capable of handling a canoe alone, you should enlist help in lifting it to your shoulders. The two-person lift is identical to the one-person lift, except that your helper stands next to you, behind the yoke, and you stand slightly in front of it. The canoe should be supported on the thighs of both you and your partner prior to raising it into position. Your hands will be forward of the yoke and your partner's will be behind it. At a mutually agreed upon signal, flip the canoe, with the help of your partner, up onto your shoulders.

For a completely effortless pickup, try the three-person lift. This is identical to the two-person lift, except you have an additional person. Position yourself at the yoke and have one helper stand at the bow thwart and another helper at the stern thwart. Again, you should all be on the same side of the canoe. All lift together. Nothing could be simpler.

END LIFT

The end lift is an easy way for one or two people to get a heavy canoe up.

PROCEDURE

Stand at the right rear of the canoe, facing the stern. Reach across with your right hand and grasp the left gunwale near the stern seat. Grab the right gunwale with your left hand (figure 13a). Now just roll the canoe over on its front end (figure 13b) and lift the tail in the air (figure 13c). While holding the canoe high, bow on the ground, shuffle yourself forward into the yoke. If you have a helper, let him or her hold the canoe up while you snuggle into the yoke.

The end pickup is popular with persons who for one reason or

FIGURE 13a. *The End Lift*. Step 1.

FIGURE 13b. Step 2.

FIGURE 13c. Step 3.

another don't feel confident using the standard side lift. Although lifting a canoe by one end is accepted practice, it is not good canoeing technique, mainly because the end in contact with the ground gets chewed up. Use this method on grass if you like, but avoid it in rocky areas—unless, of course, you want to fit a new deck plate to your canoe after every few trips.

TWO-PERSON CARRIES

RACING CARRY

Each paddler places his or her end of the canoe (usually, right side up) on a shoulder and cradles an arm around it for support. Once the canoe is in position, racers take off at a run and make very good time over short distances. You will like the racing carry if you have a very light, keelless canoe (keels gouge shoulders miserably, rendering this method too painful for canoes with keels).

SEAT CARRY

Turn the canoe over and place the front edge of a seat on the back of your neck. Your partner should follow suit, using the other seat. You should both wear life jackets to help pad your necks. This method works reasonably well if the distance is short and the life jackets used are the inexpensive orange horse-collar type. The newer style vest preservers don't have enough padding, and your neck suffers accordingly. The canoe used by Kruger and Waddell on their Alaskan canoe safari was equipped with a portage yoke at each end to facilitate this style of carry. While some veteran canoeists scoff at two-person carries, they are ideal under some conditions—and you don't have to impress anyone but yourself on a wilderness trip!

CANOE TUMPLINES

A tumpline consists of a wide leather or canvas strap secured to a pack or bundle. The packer places this strap just above his forehead, grabs the tumpline near his head, leans forward into the trace, and takes off down the trail. The early voyageurs carried 180 pounds and more across rugged portages using only this rig. If tumplines have a major failing, it is that they exert tremendous pressure on neck muscles, and most modern voyageurs just don't have strong enough necks to tolerate this for very long. Consequently, many canoeists use a combination of tumpline and straps on their packs. By distributing the weight between tumpline and straps, you can carry very heavy loads for short distances in relative comfort.

For years canoeists have been trying to install tumplines on their canoes to make carrying easier. Unfortunately, conventional tumplines are too rigid. When the canoe bounces up, the tump comes off your head and wraps around your neck. And when the canoe comes down, your head receives the full impact of the weight. A few years ago I began to experiment earnestly with canoe tumplines. At the time I was anticipat-

FIGURE 14a. A canoe tumpline that works!

FIGURE 14b. Ken Saelens modeling his ingeniously designed homemade tumpline.

ing an arctic canoe trip with a thirteen-mile portage. Although I was excited about the trip, I began to have nightmares about carrying my 75-pound canoe across that portage. I figured that with a tumpline, somehow I could make it. I tried rigging one using shock cords, but that didn't work—the thing kept slipping off my head. So I posed the problem to an inventive friend of mine, Ken Saelens. Ken thought a while, then attached a 24-inch length of canvas beneath the yoke of the canoe with two heavy-duty rubber ropes (figures 14a, 14b). The result was dramatic. The tumpline took about fifty percent of the weight off my shoulders while the canvas eliminated the dangerous possibility of it coming loose and possibly strangling me. In addition, the canvas was handy as a lunch tray and storage shelf for small items.

CANOE RACKS AND CARS

Each year we read about canoes which have blown off cars, causing and suffering extensive damage. This has become such a problem that some states have considered banning the carrying of boats on car tops. Fortunately for all of us, these proposals have not yet become law. After years of transporting canoes atop all sorts of vehicles, I have learned that it pays to buy the best carrying racks available. A good many people buy inexpensive suction-cup carriers, strap their canoes on, and take to the road without a second thought to the safety of their craft. The canoe owner who successfully uses these types of carriers for many years without an accident is either exceptionally cautious, unusually lucky, or a very slow driver.

Get canoe racks that bolt directly to the car's drip eaves. Avoid models that put pressure on the roof. In some cases you can buy individual mounting brackets and attach them to two-by-fours to make racks. Most avid canoeists prefer this type of arrangement. The wide weight-bearing surface of the two-by-fours keeps canoes from sliding around, and the large size of the wood cross-bars makes for very sturdy racks. If you buy separate brackets and make your own car-top carriers, make the cross-bars about 82 inches long. This length will enable you to carry two canoes comfortably. Even if you never plan to buy a second canoe, you will often need to shuttle more than one, especially if you paddle with a club. A common mistake is to make double racks about 78 inches long. Although you can easily fit two canoes on them, the sides will nearly touch; on a long drive, regardless of the care you take, the canoe hulls will come into contact. The resulting friction may remove enough material to cause serious damage to one or both canoes. This is a very real problem, especially when canoes are built of different materials—for example, aluminum and fiberglass. As an added precaution, canoes carried in pairs should have a 12-by-24 inch piece of carpet placed between them. This pad should be well secured to one of the canoes with light rope. It is also a good idea to carpet cross-bars. Sew the carpeting around the bars with heavy waxed thread. Virtually every canoe I have owned has suffered some damage from being transported on noncarpeted racks. You especially need carpeting if your canoe has wood or plastic gunwales. When you are selecting a car-top carrier, don't be misled by the gaudy appearance of chrome-plated models. Canoe racks are wet much of the time, and even good quality plated steel fittings will rust. Look for cast or machined aluminum parts. The cost will be much higher, but the service will be considerably better. For the past ten years I have been using a set of all-aluminum carriers by Quick 'N Easy and I have found these to be ideal.

FOR SAFETY'S SAKE, TIE 'EM DOWN

Most canoeists give only casual thought to securing their canoes to car-top carriers. A properly tied down canoe should show little, if any, movement, even in high winds at speeds well in excess of those legally posted. As a rule of thumb, each canoe carried should be tied down separately. This will eliminate many embarrassing problems at highway speeds. Attach a stout ¼ inch nylon rope to each car rack. Run the lines over the belly of the canoe and secure them to the other side of the rack. Tie each as close as possible to the gunwales of the canoe to prevent wind-shift. The power-cinch (see Chapter 9—Tying It All Together) is the most suitable knot and is the only one that should be used for tying down canoes. Additionally, tie two ropes to *each* end of the canoe and attach the free ends of these lines to their respective bumpers, as far apart as possible. Again, use a power-cinch. Make up a special set of nylon ropes with S-hooks at each end. It is very difficult to attach naked ropes to bumpers properly. The sharp bumper edges can easily cut even thick rope on a long auto trip if sufficient friction is generated by high winds. Caution: avoid use of rubber truck tie-downs. Although they are quite popular, they have too much stretch and can cause problems if the canoe is buffeted by wind. Some canoeists use them because they are easy to get on and off. For safety's sake, I prefer to tie 'em down. Lastly, if you cartop two canoes on one car, attach an S-hook to the center of both carriers and run each belly rope through the hook. This is in keeping with the aforementioned rule of thumb, and will also help keep paired canoes from rubbing.

SPECIAL CONSIDERATIONS WHEN CARTOPPING NONALUMINUM CANOES

Nonaluminum canoes are extremely sensitive to damage from abrasion. For this reason nylon belly ropes should be at least ⅜ of an inch in diameter. Even slight friction under ropes will cause burn or scald marks to appear on the canoe's outer skin. For wood-canvas canoes it may be wise to insert a 4-inch-wide strip of carpeting under each belly rope to prevent paint galling. You can't cinch down fiberglass or wood canoes as tightly as aluminum ones, for too much tension can pull out bow and stern fittings, or possibly even crack the canoe. When faced with high winds I make two bridles for the canoe by tying a rope completely around the hull about a foot back of each end. These ropes are then used as anchor points for front bumper lines. This keeps the stress off wood-mounted screw eyes and delicate fiberglass fittings.

WHERE'S THE PORTAGE?

Much of North America's canoe country consists of a maze of lakes connected by waterfalls, rapids, and meandering streams. In some cases you can run the rapids or walk the streams. Often you will have no recourse but to pack your canoe and gear over rugged portage trails. One of the great challenges of the wilderness is locating the proper portage. Usually this is easy enough, especially on small lakes. On large lakes with a multitude of islands, channels, and bays, good maps, a reliable compass, and a high degree of resourcefulness will be required (see Chapter 11—Wilderness Navigation, for a complete discussion of route finding). In isolated areas a portage may be marked by a blazed tree, a jutting pole, a piece of discarded wearing apparel hanging from a tree limb, or a small opening in the forest. One portage, located along the Granite River on the United States–Canadian border, requires carrying your canoe up over a steep, sheer rock face. Except for a small faded *P* painted on the rock some years ago, the portage is impossible to spot.

Locating routes around dangerous rapids and waterfalls on large rivers can be a matter of survival. On my early wilderness river trips, I was always afraid that I would miss a portage and paddle over a falls. Such fear, though common in beginners, is unfounded. Your ears quickly become attuned to the roar of perilous rapids and the gurgle of safe fast water. Usually (though not always) rapids can be heard for great distances. I especially remember the Grand Rapids on the Mattagami River in northern Ontario. I could hear those rapids nearly ten miles away when the wind was right. As the wind lessened in force, so did the sound, and when the wind blew harder the noise became louder. This waning and waxing of sound haunted me throughout the night and provided ample opportunity for me to exaggerate the size and fury of the rapids. When our party finally reached Grand Rapids, we found it to be nothing spectacular, although it was perhaps two miles long and a quarter of a mile wide. The tremendous thundering we heard was due to the great number of rapids, not their size. Your ears are a most valuable tool for detecting the dangers ahead. For this reason white-water helmets always have holes or cutouts for the ears.

On isolated northern rivers there may be nothing to mark portage trails, yet a route around impassable water often exists. Most portages are trampled into place by large animals like moose and bear, who, like you, need to get around rapids and falls. It remains for you to find these trails. Sometimes this can be difficult, as the only evidence of them may be a few broken twigs and bushes near the water's edge. Portages are most often located on the inside curves of rivers, and this is the place you should look first. When you hear the roar of rapids and see the white plumes of dancing horse-tails leaping high into the air, immediately get to the inside bend and paddle ashore. Then get out of your canoe and start looking. Walk the rapids to see if they are safe to run. If you can find no portage and the rapids look safe, proceed cautiously downstream. Sometimes a single hidden ledge can make a rapid unnavigable, and you may not be able to see the ledge until it is too late.

The absence of a portage does not mean the rapid is safe to run. Unusually high water may flood existing portages, making them impossible to find, and very low water can change channel characteristics so completely that you may paddle right by the portage without seeing it.

In some areas, especially those near James and Hudson bays, portages are so overgrown with vegetation that you may have to hack your way through a maze of brush to reach safer water at the end of the trail. Cutting paths through the bush is not in keeping with the modern wilderness ethic (Leave only footprints, take only pictures), but occasionally, for reasons of safety, you may have no choice. Fortunately for the environment, the scrubby trees you destroy will grow back quickly.

Never underestimate the power of rapids, especially if the water is high. The rule of thumb in the wilderness is If in doubt, portage! Develop your white-water skills at home, not on an isolated canoe trip where a single error can be fatal.

5.
Paddle Power!

Although paddling a canoe today is much the same as it was a century ago, better equipment and techniques have made it possible for canoeists of limited experience to successfully negotiate rapids which up until a few years ago were considered impossible. Modern canoeists use paddle strokes which are more powerful, efficient, and less demanding of energy than those used by less scientific paddlers of the past. As a result, a whole new style of canoeing has evolved—a style geared to the superbly designed responsive canoes and ultralight equipment of today.

Some of our best competitors in both white- and flat-water events have been paddling for only a few years, yet they would put a professional northwoods guide to shame. While experience is still the best teacher, you can gain a great deal from good books and watching others. It may surprise you to know that white-water canoeists often learn their basic skills in swimming pools. In fact, some very good scores in slalom competition have been posted by first-year paddlers who never saw a river before their first event. This is not to say that experience on wilderness waterways is not valuable. But you can learn to handle your canoe efficiently on the calm lakes and rivers near your home. First, however, you will have to forget much of what you learned from traditional books of the past.

EQUIPMENT FIRST—THE CANOE PADDLE

Not long ago I received a call from a canoeist who wanted to know how to repair an aluminum canoe. It seems his canoe turned broadside to the current, upset, and wrapped around a rock. Total damage included a bent keel, two bent ribs, and several pulled rivets. "How did it happen?" I asked. "Well," he replied, "We were approaching Dragon's Tooth, doing just fine, when I broke my paddle. Before I could get to the spare, she spun around and . . . well, it was all I could do to get out of there."

As you can see, being up a creek without a paddle is considerably less dangerous than being caught in the middle of a raging river without one. In either case, a cheap, poorly constructed paddle is usually at fault; good paddles seldom fail.

There are reasons besides safety to buy a quality-built paddle. You can't play a good game of hockey without skates that fit properly, and you can't make a canoe respond to your whims without a decently designed, comfortable paddle. Good paddles are not cheap, but as the case in point illustrates, this is one place where you should not try to save money. Older canoe books often gave detailed instructions on how to make a paddle. Today we have little use for such information, for the age of technology has produced a wide variety of unbelievably strong, nearly break-proof paddles.

WHAT ABOUT STYLE?

You will need the same amount of effort to propel your canoe regardless of the length, width, or style of your paddle. The question really is how you want the work distributed. To move your canoe at a given speed will require more strokes with a narrow-bladed paddle than with a wider one, though you will expend more effort in pushing the wider blade through the water. Precise maneuvering in rapids demands that your canoe respond quickly to your paddle. Consequently, canoe enthusiasts

FIGURE 15. *A Few of the Excellent Paddles Currently Available* (left to right):

1. Sports Equipment Grabber
2. Blue Hole
3. Iliad
4. Norse
5. Sawyer Kruger model
6. Nona
7. Cadorette 8-inch deluxe
8. Cadorette 8-inch standard
9. Cadorette (Advertising mock-up. A useful child's paddle.)
10. Cadorette 6¾-inch standard
11. Clement 268 DRT
12. Clement 229 SRT
13. Old Town
14. Smoker Craft (camp paddle)
15. Grumman Masterlite
16. Hauthaway
17. L. L. Bean, Inc. Guide model

(See Appendix D for manufacturers' addresses, paddle characteristics, and paddle costs.)

usually choose paddles with blades at least 7½ inches wide. And since the river canoeist in shallow water is often faced with the impossibility of getting more than about half his blade in the water, the paddle style should reflect this difficulty.

The maximum possible surface area at the paddle tip should be exposed to the water without making the paddle awkward to handle. This means the edges of the river paddle blade should be fairly straight, not gracefully rounded and tapered like the typical lake paddle. If the choice rests between two paddles of similar surface area, select the model with the shortest but widest blade. This does not mean that 10- to 12-inch-wide "banjo" blades are most desirable. Although some extra-wide paddles have enjoyed success at the hands of professional racers, they tend to be somewhat awkward to use, especially in white water. Most canoeists prefer a blade width of about 8 to 9 inches.

The biggest objection to the somewhat squarish racing type paddle is the continual abuse which the corners receive. A shallow, rocky stream can really destroy a square tip in short order. If you select the square tip (and most serious canoeists do), invest in some epoxy (not polyester) resin and some 4-inch-wide fiberglass cloth with bound edges. Use this material to glass and reglass the paddle to about 2 inches back from the tip. Don't overdo it, though, because epoxy adds weight to the paddle. Fiberglassing is unbelievably easy. Just follow the directions on the can and don't let the messy look of the drying paddle scare you. Hardened glass cuts and sands easily, and a proper job will be hardly noticeable.

WOOD, GLASS, OR ALUMINUM?

Except for white-water use, where paddles really take a beating, wood is still the best choice. Not only is it more pleasing to look at; it doesn't get as cold or as hot as synthetic materials. However, where areas are certain to be shallow and rocky, one of the glass-blade, aluminum-shaft models might be the best choice. Unfortunately, to create a really great paddle out of epoxy glass and aluminum is expensive. The further one gets from sawing a simple paddle from a single board, the more expensive the process. For example, a cheap wood paddle has a shaft that is somewhat oval in cross-section, with the largest diameter of the oval in the same plane as the blade, because the paddle is cut from a single board. This flattened cross-section in the wrong direction makes these cheapies a pain to paddle with, and certainly does not add to their strength. More expensive paddles have a round shaft, which requires more processing than the flattened shaft. This is a distinct improvement, but top-of-the-line models always have an oval shaft which runs at ninety degrees to the paddle blade, thus following the natural contours of the hand.

HOW LONG SHOULD A PADDLE BE?

Except when used by the lone paddler in an open canoe, paddles of any great length have all but disappeared from the modern canoe scene. Racers paddling sleek, low-to-the-water hulls commonly choose paddle lengths of 54 to 58 inches, or even less. Most paddlers of stock model canoes which ride relatively high in the water may choose lengths up to about 60 inches—but seldom much more. Since a canoe will move more rapidly when given several short, powerful strokes as opposed to a few long, gliding ones, an extra foot of lumber in your hands will only weaken your stroke.

Choosing a paddle according to your height or reach has no rational basis, because you sit in a canoe—you don't stand in it. And since some of us have long upper torsos while others have short ones, choosing a paddle that comes to the eyes, nose, or throat has little, if any, relationship to actual need. Simply put, buy a paddle with enough length to do the job without a bunch of wood sticking out of the water when the blade is submerged. And you *do* want to submerge the blade—*all* of it! Buying a long-bladed paddle and leaving six inches of blade out of the water is profoundly wasteful, from the standpoint of both energy and wood. Besides, it's poor style.

WHAT ABOUT CONSTRUCTION?

Canoeists of competence universally agree that laminated paddles are best. Good laminated models (and I don't mean those $3.98 pseudo-racing types stacked helter-skelter in a barrel at your local discount store) are generally about a quarter of an inch thick. They derive their strength from the fact that they are comprised of *good* laminations. For some nebulous reason, many writers recommend flexibility in paddle blades, claiming that rigid blades transmit a shock to the shoulders with each stroke. Good laminated paddles do have some small degree of flexibility—but very little. Racers push their craft unbelievable distances for unbelievable hours, and their paddles are about as flexible as a policeman's nightstick.

As for paddle grips, buy what suits you. Many serious canoeists prefer the T-style grip, as it gives better control. But the oval or pear grip is still popular and is probably more rugged.

CUSTOMIZING AN INEXPENSIVE PADDLE

Many of us who canoe are forced to operate on limited budgets. Admittedly, the "canoe budget" can become a status symbol—an approach to martyrdom and a complete reversal of the motorboat ethic which requires one to keep up with the Johnsons, the Evinrudes, or the Mercurys. Those of us with motorboat aspirations and canoe budgets must learn to live with less-than-superior equipment. This is usually reflected in our paddles.

Most commonly met on wilderness waterways is the $3.98 spruce special. This paddle is not only heavy and cumbersome; it breaks almost without provocation. However, with a little ingenuity and effort, it can be converted into a sturdy, beautiful, and efficient paddle. Most $3.98 specials have a blade about 5 to 6 inches wide. With a table saw, cut off both sides of the blade parallel to the shaft, as shown in figure 16. Then get an old, broken paddle and cut and split the end as shown. Glue the blade segments to the new paddle and trim as illustrated. The entire blade should be thinned to a uniform thickness of 3/16 to $\frac{1}{4}$ of an inch and each side covered with fiberglass and epoxy resin. Because inexpensive paddle shafts are inherently weak, it is almost mandatory that they be covered with fiberglass.

THE GREAT VARNISH MYTH

A varnished grip is supposed to give you blisters. Most racing paddles are dipped in or sprayed with a quality varnish. Racers paddle all day. Racers seldom get blisters. Racers don't wear gloves. Need I say more?

The key to a blisterless canoe trip rests in the quality and smoothness of the finish, rather than the type of finish applied. Whatever you

FIGURE 16. *Customizing an Inexpensive Paddle*

1. Make cuts along dotted line as indicated.
2. Throw away pieces D, E, and F.
3. Attach pieces A and B to the inexpensive paddle with epoxy glue and finish to assume shape of new paddle.
4. Make T-grip from 1¼-inch diameter wooden dowel, finish to 4¼-inch length, and install in place of old grip.
5. Fiberglass entire blade after thinning to ¼-inch, and glass shaft to point f or beyond. (Note: paddle shaft of new paddle will still be oval in the wrong direction. However, judicious sanding and fiberglassing to point f will increase the comfort of the shaft somewhat.)

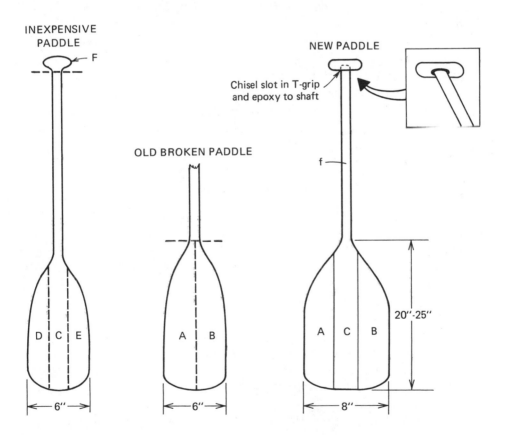

use, sand and steelwool the final coat until the wood has a distinctly
silky feel. This will protect both the paddle and your hands. However,
if you feel the need to adhere to the ways of historic canoeists, the shaft
and grip can be left unprotected. To many, a finishless or linseed oil–
rubbed paddle is indicative of an expert canoeist.

PADDLE STROKES

The following canoe strokes have been learned and perfected over
the past twenty-five years. However, don't take that too seriously, since
up until about eight years ago, according to an "efficient" canoe-paddling
course I enrolled in, I did everything wrong—in spite of the fact that I
could paddle a canoe straight, turn effectively, and do a whole lot of
other impressive things.

Experience is not always the best teacher. Now that I have seen the
error of my ways, I will pass on some of the things I have learned. If
you're a canoeist from the old school, you may shake your head in dis-
belief and wonder at the new strokes. Nevertheless, they are more powerful and efficient than the older variations, and white-water paddlers are
in complete agreement that you should master them if you intend to
paddle rapids of even moderate difficulty.

THE FORWARD (OR BOW) STROKE

To make the forward stroke most effective, reach as far forward as
you can (but don't lunge). Put the paddle into the water at least two
feet in front of your body. At the start of the stroke, the top arm is bent
and the lower arm is straight. At the end of the stroke, the positions are
reversed. Keep your top hand low—below your chin and *push*. Most of
the power in the stroke should come from pushing with the top hand,
not from pulling with the bottom. The stroke is lightning-fast and powerful, and the control is in the top hand. Paddle parallel to the keel, as
close to the canoe as possible, and don't bring your lower hand back
beyond your hip. Bringing the paddle farther back than necessary
wastes energy and power. In fact, carrying a stroke too far back actually
slows the canoe down. This is because a paddle is not really pushed
through the water; rather, the canoe moves forward to the place where
the stroke began. So if a paddle is brought back beyond the vertical (blade

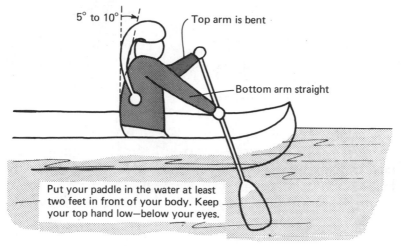

5° to 10°

Top arm is bent

Bottom arm straight

Put your paddle in the water at least two feet in front of your body. Keep your top hand low—below your eyes.

START OF FORWARD STROKE

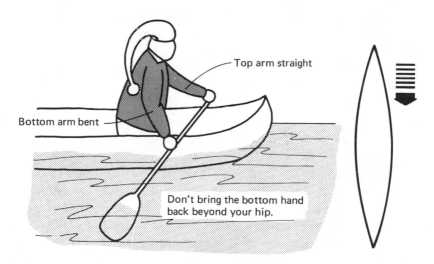

Top arm straight

Bottom arm bent

Don't bring the bottom hand back beyond your hip.

FINISH OF FORWARD STROKE

FIGURE 17. *The Forward Stroke*

pulled upward in the water behind the paddler), the canoe will be forced
down in the water, and this will cause a drag on the canoe's forward
motion.

The most common mistake beginners make is to paddle across their
bodies. It is important that the paddle shaft be *perpendicular* to the
water, not angled out from the canoe. To effect this, reach far across your
body with your top hand and twist your shoulders into the stroke. For
greatest power, paddle from a sitting position. Only when you are in
heavy rapids or running waves should you kneel.

Most canoeists dismiss the forward stroke as something anyone
can do. The truth is most of us do it wrong, and some cling to bad habits
for many years. A canoe spends almost all of its time going forward;
therefore, greater effort should go into paddling it more efficiently.

THE BACK STROKE

Most canoeists pick up the back stroke out of necessity when a large
rock looms ahead and they need to avoid it. Other names given to this
stroke are help!, good grief!, and @##&**! It is the exact opposite of
the forward stroke, and all comments made about that stroke apply here.

Start the stroke where the bow (forward) stroke ends, and end the
stroke where the bow stroke starts. Confused? Well, this is one stroke
that comes naturally.

There is an alternate form of the back stroke that is favored by some
white-water paddlers. Rotate your top hand and paddle shaft 180 degrees, so you are looking at your fingers rather than your knuckles.
Power is thus provided by pushing your top hand back toward you rather
than pulling it. Although not necessarily more powerful than the conventional back stroke, this variation allows you to turn your body and look
backward in the direction you are paddling. It permits instant transfer
to the very important *draw* stroke without sacrificing control (a must
when executing the *back ferry*—the canoeist's most useful river tactic.
See Chapter 6—On the Water—for a discussion of this technique).

THE DRAW STROKE

The draw stroke is the most important turning stroke. A powerful
draw makes the bow person an active navigator rather than just a horse-

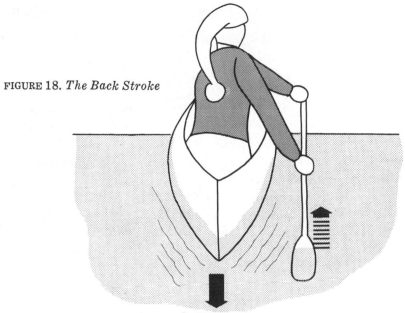

FIGURE 18. *The Back Stroke*

Canoe moves in
this direction

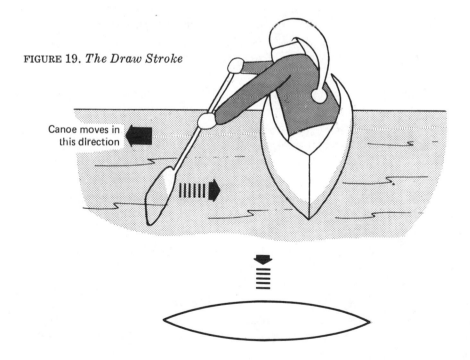

FIGURE 19. *The Draw Stroke*

Canoe moves in
this direction

power machine (figure 19). The draw stroke is perhaps the most important stroke in white water. Avoid the challenge of white-water wilderness trips until you can perform this stroke quickly, powerfully, and
precisely.

For maximum power the draw should be executed from a kneeling
position. Reach out as far from the gunwale as you can—don't be afraid
to lean the canoe. Keep your top hand high and draw the paddle quickly
and powerfully toward you. When the paddle reaches within 6 inches of
the canoe, slice it out and draw again.

It is important to realize that the force of the water under the canoe
has a righting effect on the canoe, so you can lean way out on this stroke
and apply power with your whole body. The canoe *will not* tip over. The
righting effect ceases, however, when the paddle is no longer in motion,
so you must recenter your weight the moment you take the power off
the paddle. The modern trend of running rapids is to run them as slowly
as possible, as this gives you time to respond correctly and results in
less damage to your canoe if it strikes a rock. Rudder motions are useful
for turning only if you have forward speed, which is why the draw is so
important. Although commonly used by both paddlers, the draw is most
effective in the bow. It is not uncommon on white-water streams to hear,
off in the distance, a desperate stern paddler screaming *"Draw . . .
draw!"* to a frustrated bow partner.

THE PRYAWAY STROKE

The pryaway is used for moving the canoe away from your paddling
side. It can be used effectively by either paddler, but is most often used
in the stern. It is a modern version of the old *pushover* stroke, although
considerably more powerful. Slice the paddle into the water as far under
the canoe as possible. With a deft, powerful motion, pry the paddle over
the top of the gunwale. After some practice you will find that it is easier
and faster to use an underwater rather than an aerial recovery for your
paddle. The mechanics of this will come naturally after a short time.
Unlike the draw, the pryaway has no righting effect on the canoe; hence
it is important that you keep your weight well centered throughout the
stroke. Since the pryaway is very powerful, it should not be used in
shallow water where the paddle might catch on a rock and overturn the
canoe. In shallow water the bow person should use a *cross draw*.

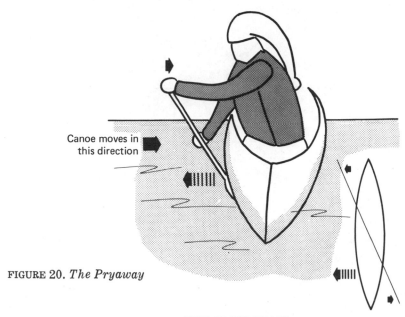

FIGURE 20. *The Pryaway*

THE CROSS-DRAW

The cross-draw, as the name implies, is a draw stroke crossed over to the other side of the canoe. It is used in water too shallow to effect a proper pryaway.

Pivot at the waist, swing the paddle over the bow (the stroke cannot be done in the stern) . . . and *draw!* Don't change your grip on the paddle. Angle the paddle forward so that it is nearly parallel to the water. Force water under and in front of the bow. As with the pryaway, keep your weight centered, as the cross draw has no stabilizing effect on the canoe.

A bow person who can correctly perform draw, cross-draw, and pryaway strokes is indispensable in white water. If you are paddling stern in fast water you will damage your canoe less if you trust your bow person's ability. The stern person is captain of the ship in calm water, but the bow paddler is the chief navigator and has the major responsibility in rapids.

Like many veteran canoeists, it was difficult for me to learn to trust my bow paddler. I, back in the stern, *always* made the route (not necessarily *right*) decisions. Then one day while the canoe was flipped over on its back I began to look at the number and placement of dents which had accumulated over the years. Quite amazingly, almost all the dents were forward of the beam, and most of them were on the left side (my

Canoe moves in
this direction

FIGURE 21. *The Cross Draw*

weaker side). On the next white-water trip I paddled bow and put my neophyte partner in the stern. Amazingly, the canoe struck only a few rocks, mostly with the tail, although I must admit that directional control from the back was at times somewhat lacking. The moral, of course, is, first train your bow paddler—then trust him or her. The rewards will be many.

THE J-STROKE

A canoe moving forward has a tendency to veer away from the side on which the stern person is paddling. When paddling backward the reverse is true. The J-stroke is used to keep a canoe on a straight course. It is the stern person's stroke when paddling forward, and a reverse form of it (the *reverse-j*) is used by the bow, or by a solo, paddler, when paddling backward. Begin the J like a typical forward stroke, but shortly after the paddle enters the water, start changing its pitch ever so slightly by turning the thumb of the top hand down and away from your body. As the paddle is pushed forward through the water, continue to increase the pitch progressively. At the completion of the stroke, the thumb of the top hand should be pointing straight down, placing the paddle in a rudder position. If at the end of the stroke additional correction is needed, force the paddle out from the canoe in a prying fashion. If no further correction is necessary, take the paddle out of the water and repeat the stroke.

There are many variations of the *J-stroke,* and each canoeist develops a style that suits him or her best. Many very good paddlers finish the stroke by prying the paddle shaft off the gunwales or their thighs. Completing the stroke with a pry is frowned upon in some circles, since it abuses paddles (and gunwales). However, it is a very efficient form of the J, and most white-water canoeists use it. Another variation of the J, used almost exclusively by paddlers of decked slalom canoes, is the *thumbs-up J.* This stroke is begun as a powerful forward stroke, upon completion the thumb of the top hand is turned up quickly, snapping the paddle into a rudder position. A fast pry off the gunwales straightens the canoe. The result is a very powerful and relaxing stroke which permits you to paddle long distances without tiring. Some veteran canoeists scoff at this stroke because they believe the mark of a good paddler is the ability to keep a canoe traveling on a straight course without veering. Both the thumbs-up and pry form of the J cause the canoe to veer slightly back and forth as it is paddled.

FIGURE 22. *The J-Stroke*

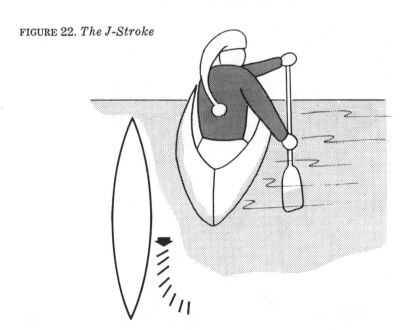

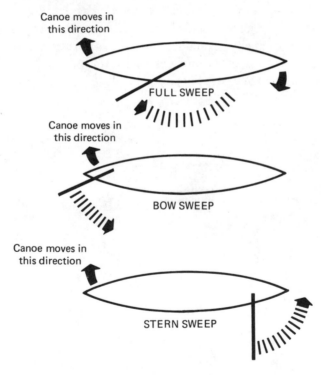

Canoe moves in
this direction

FULL SWEEP

Canoe moves in
this direction

BOW SWEEP

Canoe moves in
this direction

STERN SWEEP

FIGURE 23. *The Sweep Stroke*

Many champion white-water canoeists use the thumbs-up J for paddling their skittish, decked fiberglass boats. When gliding quietly among the lily pads, the traditional J is best. But in heavy rapids and waves the newer, more efficient variations are often better.

THE SWEEP STROKE

Sweep strokes are used to turn the canoe in a wide arc, either toward or away from your paddling side. Both the draw and pryaway are more efficient, and if you have mastered these you will probably use the sweep only occasionally.

Bow Sweep

Place your paddle in the water far forward, nearly touching the bow. Sweep the paddle outward in a wide arc and stop when it is perpendicular to the canoe.

Stern Sweep

Place your paddle in the water at a right angle to the canoe. Sweep in a wide arc all the way back to the stern.

THE STERN PRY

The stern pry is not a stroke; it is a powerful technique for turning the canoe toward the stern person's paddle side. It is similar to the pryaway, except it is begun farther back. A common error is shown in figure 24.

THE SCULLING DRAW

The sculling draw is an impressive-looking stroke. It is not one that you need to learn right away, as you can use the draw to perform the same function. However, it is a nice stroke in its place, and that place is in parallel landing to a shore line in water too shallow to get a good draw.

Place the paddle in the water in a draw position at a comfortable

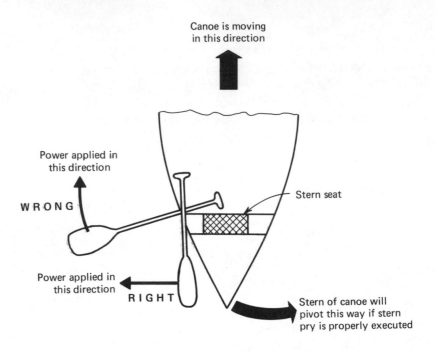

Canoe is moving
in this direction

Power applied in
this direction

WRONG

Stern seat

Power applied in
this direction

RIGHT

Stern of canoe will
pivot this way if stern
pry is properly executed

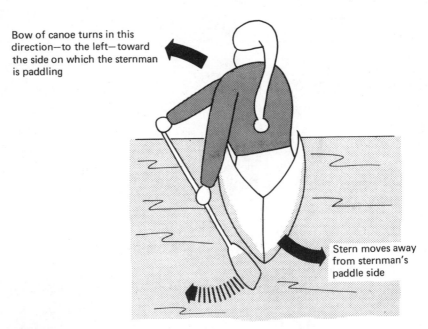

Bow of canoe turns in this
direction—to the left—toward
the side on which the sternman
is paddling

Stern moves away
from sternman's
paddle side

FIGURE 24. *The Stern Pry*

Canoe will move
in this direction

FIGURE 25. *The Sculling Draw*

distance from the canoe. Turn the leading edge of the paddle about forty-five degrees away from the canoe, and while holding this blade angle pull the paddle backward through the water for a distance of about two feet. Then reverse the angle of the leading edge ninety degrees from the previous direction and, while holding this new blade angle, push the paddle forward about 2 feet to complete the stroke. The sculling draw is sometimes called the *figure 8* stroke because the paddle appears to describe an *8* in the water. This is not really accurate, however, since the paddle is pulled straight fore and aft, and only the blade angle is changed.

THE MINNESOTA SWITCH

Some early Indian tribes adopted an unorthodox but very efficient method of keeping a canoe on course. Both paddlers used short, powerful forward strokes to propel the canoe, and when they wanted to change direction they would merely flip their paddles over the canoe and change paddle sides. This would give the stern person leverage on the other side, so no correctional stroke (like the J) was necessary. The net effect, of course, was that the canoe traveled a somewhat erratic path in the water. The white man, feeling that swtching sides wasted energy and efficiency, adopted the J-stroke, which is in common use today.

About thirty years ago some professional Minnesota racers tried the switching technique in competition. The results were dramatic. Not only could a canoe be paddled faster by switching sides every six strokes or so, but it could also be paddled farther, since the paddlers became less tired. Over the years the Minnesota switch grew in popularity, and today virtually all professional racers use it instead of the J-stroke. Al Button, America's medal-winning white-water champion, used it at the white-water world championships in 1975 to take a bronze medal. I asked Al if European paddlers were showing any interest in the switching technique. "When I took third place, they showed some interest," he replied. "If I had been fortunate enough to take a first, everybody would have been using it within a year!"

To an old-school canoeist the Minnesota switch is a prime example of poor technique, mostly because the canoe does not travel a straight-line course. But it *is* efficient, especially on wilderness trips when you want to make good time against big incoming rollers on a windswept lake. Kruger and Waddell used the Minnesota switch almost exclusively on their voyage to the Bering Sea. Their cadence was approximately sixty strokes per minute, with a switch after each six to eight strokes.

PADDLING ALONE

For many, paddling alone is the most satisfying way to travel. With the paddler at the center of the canoe, the ends are light enough to rise and fall easily with waves. The lone canoeist who is a competent paddler is well equipped to handle most rough-water situations. The biggest problem with paddling a canoe alone is that of making good time on flat water (no rapids). The single canoeist lacks the stabilizing effect of a partner, and thus must make up for it by using a very powerful J-stroke. The net result is that speed is sacrificed for directional control. You can make up for this somewhat by adopting the Minnesota switch, or you can use a long, double-bladed, kayak-type paddle. In calm water you can pack your gear around the bow seat and paddle from the stern. This will reduce the canoe's tendency to veer away from your paddle side because your stroke will be closer to the keel line. In rough water, however, you will want to kneel at or slightly back of center, and this will become tiring in a short time. Many lone canoeists prefer a variation of the high kneeling, or racing, position. To assume this posture, place your buttocks against the stern thwart and the knee closest to your paddle side on the canoe's bottom. Extend your other foot forward for support, keeping the leg almost straight. Make sure you have a soft kneeling pad.

LEANING THE CANOE

It would be unfair to leave the subject of paddling without mentioning the technique of leaning the canoe to make a turn. To make a gradual turn lean the canoe (an inch or two is sufficient) to the *outside* of the turn (the reverse of what you would do on a bicycle). If you hold the lean the canoe will cut a nice arc in the *opposite* direction of the lean. Pro racers do almost all their turning by this method and lone paddlers of decked slalom canoes often use a counter lean to help keep their skittish boats from turning away from their paddling side. Caution: Don't use this technique for quick turns in rapids—you will upset the canoe!

It is beyond the scope of this book to present a complete course in paddling. If you want to learn more, join a canoe club and get some first-hand instruction. Also, read the excellent books on technique listed in Appendix A.

POLING THE CANOE

Although poling has long been part of the canoeist's art, it is seldom used by modern wilderness paddlers—possibly because most are not familiar with its technique. Recently, however, there has been a revival of interest in canoe poling, and championship events are now held each year.

Poling is usually (though not always) done by one person. The poler assumes a standing position in a place that will trim the downstream end of the canoe slightly down—forward of the center thwart when descending streams, and behind it when ascending them. Modern polers favor a strong, lightweight, aluminum pole about twelve feet long. Using quick, coordinated jabs, they can ascend streams with strong currents and shallow, moderate rapids; or they can carefully pick their way downstream, snubbing their poles to avoid obstacles.

Poling is a skill that requires coordination and much practice. An upstream pole in the morning followed by an afternoon downstream

paddle or float is an ideal way to see the near wilderness without the necessity of organizing and running an auto shuttle. If you are interested in learning more about this interesting method of propelling a canoe, write to the A.C. Mackenzie River Company, P.O. Box 9301, Richmond Heights Station, Saint Louis, Missouri 63117. The Mackenzie River Company can provide you with a pole, a book, and even personalized on-the-river instruction.

CANOE SAILING

From the standpoint of sheer fun, few things rival a canoe under sail. Several companies manufacture excellent sail rigs which can be easily adapted to almost any canoe. A sail makes your canoe a multi-purpose boat, permitting you to enjoy it even on crowded, close-to-home lakes and reservoirs. Most wilderness canoeists just don't give enough thought to the values of a sail. The early voyageurs sailed their birch bark canoes quite regularly, and later wood-canvas freight canoes were commonly equipped with mast steps and bars for sails.

On a recent trip to James Bay, we fought wind and driving rain for ten straight days without a break. At one point in the trip, we covered only twelve miles in three days. On another day sixteen hours of strenuous, continuous paddling were required to cross twenty-mile long Mattagami Lake, just south of Smoky Falls, Ontario. When we finally entered the very large Moose River, we knew we would have to fight the prevailing north wind for more than a hundred miles to reach James Bay. Then a miraculous change of weather occurred. The wind shifted completely to the south, providing us with a steady tail wind of perhaps twenty knots. We quickly fashioned sails and put to sea easily covering the hundred-mile distance to Moosonee in just fifteen hours! Shortly after we arrived at our destination, the wind reversed itself again. Our sail had given us the edge to play the weather odds and win.

The best and easiest way to rig a sail for a wilderness canoe is to use two stout 8-foot poles and a rain-fly or poncho. Lay the fly or poncho on the ground and roll up the poles from each end as you would a scroll.

FIGURE 26. Going upstream or downstream in shallow water is much easier with a pole than with a paddle. The canoe is an 18-foot Grumman in Okefenokee Swamp. (*Photo courtesy of Grumman Co.*)

In practice, the bow person holds the rig against the gunwales and supports the base of the poles with his or her feet. By opening and closing the scroll-like sail to catch the wind, you can control the speed of the canoe. You can also change the direction of the sail somewhat, allowing you to tack slightly. It is not a good idea to tie makeshift sails in place on loaded wilderness canoes. A heavily loaded canoe can easily get out of control in a high wind and capsize, throwing you overboard while it keeps on plowing down the lake. You may find yourself not only in the water in a running sea, but canoeless as well. Hand-held sails work well enough for most situations. If you prefer a sturdier, more permanent arrangement, install a mast step and bar and do it right. Incidentally, if you use a nylon fly for sailing, make sure you remove every trace of bark and roughness from your sail poles. I once completely destroyed a very nice nylon fly by sailing many miles in a strong wind using rough poles. When I took my fly down, it looked as if moths had been gnawing along its length! It was impossible to repair.

CATAMARANED CANOES

For greater stability on rough water or while sailing, some authorities recommend that you "catamaran" a pair of similar canoes. To prevent water buildup between the two craft, you are generally advised to use strong poles to separate the canoes about four feet at the bow and six feet at the stern. If poles are securely lashed to the canoes and a large square sail is hoisted, the rig will make reasonably good time in a strong tail wind. However, running at an angle to the wind (tacking) is nearly impossible with such an outfit, and any degree of maneuverability is out of the question. Moreover, an important advantage of the single canoe over more stable, paired craft is its ability to roll with the side thrust of waves—an ability which is completely negated by the rigid, unyielding design of the catamaran. In short, paired canoes respond poorly to the pitch of a rough sea, and consequently tend to ship water readily.

An additional concern is the danger of a rope lashing or wood crossbrace breaking, and if this happens in a good blow, a dunking is inevitable. I have used paired canoes for casual downwind sailing and for placid-water recreational paddling, but I consider them downright dangerous for general rough-water use—with or without sails. A well-

FIGURE 27. From the standpoint of sheer fun, few things rival a canoe under sail. The canoe is a 16-foot Old Town Wahoo. (*Photo courtesy of Old Town Canoe Co.*)

designed canoe will weather out six-foot waves if paddled by a team of experts. Catamaran-rigged canoes, on the other hand, even if securely braced and tied, are almost sure to break apart under these conditions.

When a sudden squall blows up and the waves grow to impressive heights, you will do best to put your faith in proper canoeing techniques. If this fails, hang onto your swamped canoe and trust your life jacket.

OUTBOARD MOTORS AND CANOES

Outboard motors have lost favor with modern wilderness canoeists. The noise and smell of gasoline just can't compete with the silence and grace of the paddle. Many of the more popular canoe areas are now completely closed to motor traffic, and each year additional acreage is placed into "paddle only" zones. Nevertheless, motors are still permitted on most wilderness waterways, and there is no doubt that, even with their additional weight, plus gas, they make a trip much easier.

You can put a motor on almost any canoe, but long canoes with big keels are best. Many of the new three- to five-horsepower motors are extremely light and work very well when side-mounted on a typical two-ended canoe. There is little problem in using side-mounted motors; in fact, they are actually easier to use than transom-mounted models because you don't have to reach directly behind your body to operate the controls or to steer. The major failing of side mounts occurs in rapids and waves, where the out-of-balance canoe can flip over if the operator is not extremely careful to maintain control.

You can get along very nicely with a side mount if you use good judgment. However, if you plan to use a motor frequently, you should consider buying a special transom-equipped canoe designed especially for stern mounting. Select a model with a short transom above the water line and a completely formed stern below. Such a canoe will respond more positively to the motor than one with a chopped end, and will rise and fall more easily in large waves. Moreover, it will paddle almost as well as a conventional canoe. Caution: should you upset with a motor-equipped canoe, your motor may drag the stern several feet below the water, leaving the lighter bow end perched high, like a half-surfaced torpedo. It may be very difficult for you to get a rig like this to shore by yourself, even on a moderately choppy lake. You will need all the flotation possible to increase the canoe's buoyancy; hence, you should have your watertight packs well secured in the canoe. You should also have at least one long line attached (a painter) to the canoe so that you can pull it behind you while you swim to shore. Two very good friends of mine nearly lost their lives on Minnesota's Namakan Lake when their motor-equipped canoe overturned. Fortunately they were in the water only about fifteen minutes before a passing fisherman came to their aid.

6.
On the Water

Sometimes luck will get you through a difficult white-water passage or across a dangerous running sea, but more often than not a lucky paddler is a good paddler. Unfortunately, in the process of becoming good, a spill or two, or even three, is inevitable. Although competent canoeists question those who tip frequently, they wonder about those who have never tipped at all. Your safety on wilderness trips depends in large measure on your ability to respond correctly to dangerous situations. Proper responses can only be learned from practice. "Upsetting" experiences have educational value, and your survival in rapids can well depend on your white-water education.

LOADING THE CANOE

Canoes should be loaded in the water, not on land. Standing in or placing heavy loads in canoes half out of water can bend aluminum and break wood and fiberglass keels and bottoms. Occasionally you may have no alternative but to load your canoe on land. At these times especially good judgment will be required to prevent severe damage to your canoe.

A canoe almost always handles better when loaded dead level. Neither the bow nor the stern should be higher. If an uneven distribution of weight is unavoidable, the lesser of two evils is to lighten the bow. But a light bow will give you problems in a following sea since the heavier stern will lack sufficient freeboard to keep the waves out. In rapids, directional control will be reduced by burying one end. With the front end high you may successfully negotiate large standing waves, but you will lose this advantage when you pile up on a rock because you can't maneuver. So wherever possible load dead level, and keep the weight as close to the center and as low as possible in the canoe. This is one reason why Duluth packs (see Chapter 10—The Necessities) are preferred for wilderness tripping. A fully loaded Duluth pack comes only a few inches above the gunwales in a canoe of proper depth.

WAVES AND RUNNING SEAS

On most wilderness canoe trips high winds and large waves will be encountered. It is not always possible to put ashore when these conditions develop; you may have to remain at sea until a suitable landing place can be found. As waves grow in size, keeping water out of the canoe will become a problem, especially if the craft is heavily loaded. To prevent the canoe from swamping, the ends must be lightened. This is best accomplished by moving paddlers closer together, away from the bow and stern. If you stow your load close to the yoke, there will be ample space for the bow person to move back of the bow seat and the stern person to move forward of the stern seat. It is important to realize, however, that when paddlers move closer together directional control is reduced, because paddle leverage is decreased. Where a high degree of maneuverability is required, you would probably be wisest to stay on your seat (or kneel) and load as close to the center of the canoe as possible. Use a splash cover if you plan to run heavy rapids.

You can reduce the canoe's tendency to knife through incoming waves by paddling into them at about a thirty-degree angle. This technique, called *quartering*, exposes more surface area of the canoe to the wave, thus giving the bow more lift.

To maintain good forward speed when paddling into waves, you need a powerful stroke that transfers *all* of your energy into forward motion; you cannot afford to waste power steering the canoe. When the wind is in your face and each succeeding roller dashes your canoe about, this is the time to use the Minnesota switch (see Chapter 5). *Both* paddlers must be well practiced in the switching technique. Playing dropsy with your paddle while negotiating four-foot waves or changing paddle sides at the wrong time is an invitation to disaster.

If there is a strong tail wind and maintaining directional control becomes a problem, you can rig a "sea anchor" by attaching a large cooking pot to your twenty-foot-long stern painter. The painter should be removed from its customary attachment point at the stern and rigged as a harness around the canoe, so that the anchor will pull from beneath the keel. When the pot is thrown overboard, it fills with water and keeps the canoe running straight with the wind.

Although controlling a canoe on a windblown lake can be difficult, a pair of competent paddlers can usually get along quite nicely by using proper paddling techniques. On the other hand, a solo canoeist caught in a heavy sea might well use a sea anchor to advantage.

TOWING

Accepting a tow from a passing motorboat is perhaps the biggest *faux pas* the modern canoeist can commit. It's sort of like eating garlic just before a visit to the dentist or giving your wife something for the house on her birthday. Being towed is a conscious admission that motorboats are better!

Fortunately, I have never had to accept a tow—but I have towed others. Towing a canoe presents no problem as long as you rig a towing bridle. This is most important, as the bow end of the canoe will submarine if you don't keep it up. Even if your tow rope can be attached close to the water line, a towing harness is best, as it takes the strain off the painter attachment ring or link.

To make a towing bridle tie your tow rope around the canoe's hull, winding it through the front seat supports so it won't slip forward when tension is applied. Knot the rope directly under the keel. This is exactly like installing a sea anchor, only the harness is attached at the bow end. A properly rigged canoe can be towed at nearly full throttle (I've seen powerboats buzzing along at more than twenty-five miles an hour pulling harnessed canoes).

EVASIVE TACTICS

Assume you are canoeing on a river with a strong current. Directly in front of your canoe is a large rock. If you try to steer around the rock, you are likely to get caught broadside and possibly destroy your canoe. Back paddling is not the answer, for that will merely postpone the inevitable. You require a tactic that will slow the canoe down and move it sideways *at the same time*. You need a *back ferry*.

The back ferry makes use of two directional forces: the forward

FIGURE 28. *Back-Ferry to Safety* (small arrows indicate direction of paddle movement).

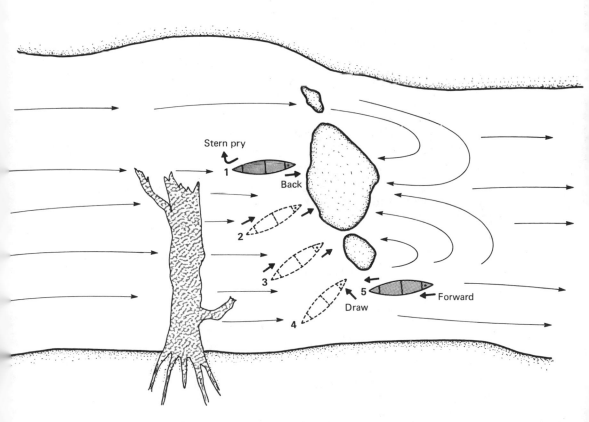

velocity of the river and the back-paddling speed of your canoe. In figure 28 the stern person is paddling on the left and begins the back ferry with a powerful stern pry. The pry is repeated until the proper angle to the current (usually about thirty degrees) is attained. The stern paddler then joins the bow person in paddling vigorously backward. The net movement, as illustrated, will be nearly sideways. The faster the river speed, the smaller the ferry angle, and vice versa.* Only experience will tell you what angle is best. You can easily increase or decrease the ferry angle by drawing or prying as needed.

On powerful, fast-flowing rivers, getting to shore quickly can be important, especially if there is a bad rapid or bouldery falls ahead. Begin the back ferry by angling your stern in the direction you want to go. Maintain the proper angle and paddle backward until your stern barely touches the shore. Then pull the bow around (using a draw or pry, whichever is appropriate) until the canoe is parallel to the land.

Landing stern first is a good habit to get into. In very swift currents bow landings can be dangerous, because a river is slowest near its edges and fastest near its center. When you nose into the slow water at the shore line, the faster main current grabs your stern and spins it downstream. If there is a sufficient current differential, you can be spun around so rapidly that you may lose your balance and possibly overturn the canoe.

Another evasive tactic based on the principle of vectors is the *forward ferry*. It is identical to the back ferry except that you spin the canoe 180 degrees and paddle forward instead of backward. This technique is used mostly by paddlers of kayaks and canoes which can turn quickly. Since the forward ferry is considerably more powerful than its backward counterpart, you can use a steeper angle to the current. You can also paddle longer distances without tiring.

On a recent Canadian river trip, my partner and I put ashore just above a bouldery falls. After about an hour of scouting, we concluded that portaging was out of the question because a high rock bluff ran for several hundred yards along the river's edge. It was apparent that a

---

* This relationship becomes *reversed* when the river speed exceeds your paddling speed. Although there is a definite trigonometric relationship between the speed of the current and the angle you should hold, in heavy rapids there is danger of swamping the canoe if you let your ferry angle get too large (greater than about forty degrees).

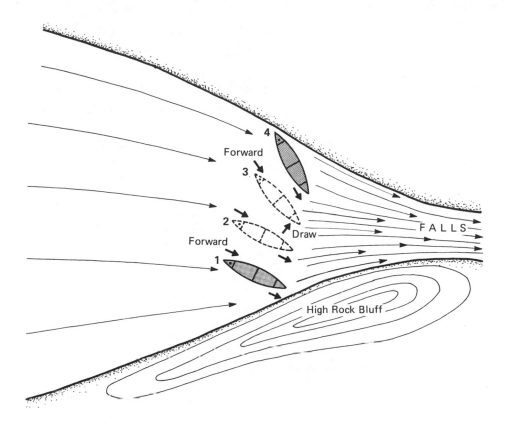

FIGURE 29. *Crossing a River Using a Forward Ferry* (arrows indicate direction of paddle movement).

portage, if one existed, was on the other bank of the hundred-yard-wide river. Somehow we would have to cross to the other side. We were within fifty feet of the falls, and the current was moving at perhaps five miles per hour. Paddling straight across was out of the question. We decided to use a very shallow angled forward ferry to test the current. Encountering no difficulty at the outset of our crossing, we steepened the angle considerably as we approached the center. We landed almost directly opposite our starting point on the other side of the river. I don't know what we would have done if this method had been unknown to us.

Although there are other white-water techniques, wilderness canoes are usually heavily loaded and thus respond very sluggishly to the paddle. You can't effectively draw a heavy canoe sideways very far to avoid obstacles. Ferrying will be one of your most useful river tactics.

RIVER FEATURES

RIVER BENDS

Whenever possible, stay on the inside of all river bends. Rivers run fastest and deepest at the outside of bends, and because of this most of the debris usually piles up there. Should you overturn and get your life jacket or clothing caught in the branches of a half-submerged tree, it could be difficult or even impossible for you to work your way free, and

FIGURE 30. *Ferrying Around a Sharp Bend*. Keep away from the outside of bends, except in low water (arrows indicate direction of paddle movement).

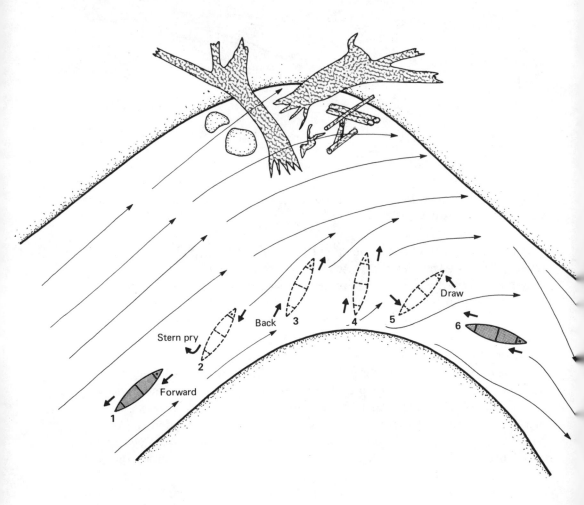

you would be lucky to escape with your life. For this reason you should seek the outside of a bend only when the water is very low or the current sluggish.

The safest way to negotiate bends is by back ferrying. Tuck your tail to the *inside* of the bend and back paddle. Although going around a bend sideways appears dangerous, it is, in fact, quite safe, for your canoe is almost perfectly aligned with the current. A slight pry or draw will quickly spin the bow downstream, putting you back on course. When you hear the thunder of rapids ahead but a curve prevents your seeing the telltale *haystacks,* get to the inside of the bend and cautiously back ferry, keeping your stern just a few feet from shore. Should the rapid prove unrunnable, a few paddle strokes will bring you to the safety of the river bank.

EDDIES ARE A CANOEIST'S FRIEND

If you have ever thrown a stick just beyond a large rock or bridge piling in a river with a good current, you have probably observed that the stick floats back upstream in the lazy current below the obstacle. This is an eddy. Paddling long stretches of difficult rapids can be exceedingly nerve-racking. The quiet water of an eddy is a convenient stopping place to rest and collect your thoughts. Polers commonly travel upstream by hopping from eddy to eddy. If the water is sufficiently deep, paddlers, too, can successfully use this technique.

Since the movement of water within an eddy is opposite to that of the river's flow, there is a current differential at the eddy's edge. This is the *eddy line,* and crossing it in strong currents can be dangerous if you are not prepared for the consequences. If you cautiously poke your bow into the slow upstream current, the main flow of the river will catch your stern and spin it quickly downstream. The result is a possible dunking. To enter an eddy bow first, you must drive powerfully forward across the eddy line. As the stern swings downstream, lean the canoe *upstream* to prevent upsetting. This forward drive requires skill and much practice, and the sluggish response of heavily loaded canoes precludes effective use of this technique except in weak or moderate currents. The safest way to enter an eddy is by back ferrying. Begin the ferry as you approach the eddy line. Set the stern into the quiet water and back paddle to safety. When you have rested sufficiently, leave the eddy at its weak lower end. If the upstream current is very strong, this may be impossible. In that case, you will have to use a fast forward ferry combined with a strong downstream lean—a sophisticated tactic requiring much practice.

When paddling difficult rapids you should proceed from eddy to eddy. At each new stopping place you can survey the conditions ahead and determine the safest course. Eddies can be used to your advantage only if you can perform a competent back ferry, so the importance of this tactic cannot be overemphasized.

CHUTES

When the river narrows sufficiently for its flow to be severely restricted, a chute of white water is formed. When the fast water racing through the chute reaches the calmer water below, its energy dissipates in the form of nearly erect standing waves called *haystacks*. A series of uniform haystacks indicates deep water and safe canoeing—that is, if they are not so large as to swamp the canoe. To help the bow lift over large haystacks, you can slow the canoe's speed by back paddling or you can quarter into the waves at a slight angle. You can also lighten the front end by putting the bow paddler behind the seat. Running a chute with large standing waves below is one of the few times when you may wish to stop and rearrange the load in your canoe.

FALLS AND DAMS

Low falls can be successfully run if there is sufficient water flowing over them and if they are not so steep as to produce a heavy back roller at their base. If after checking a falls you decide it is safe to run, pick the point of strongest water flow, align the canoe, and proceed at river speed over the falls. Upon reaching the base of the falls, dig your paddles hard and deep to climb out of the trough below.

It is almost always unsafe to run a dam—any dam, even a low one—unless, of course, part of it has broken away. The trouble with dams is not the lack of flow over them, or even the steepness of their drops. Rather, the danger lies in the well-formed back roller at their bases. The back roller is actually an extremely powerful eddy, and the upstream current of this eddy can stop you dead in your tracks. Your canoe can be flipped broadside to the current and may spin over and over like a rolling cigar, perhaps to remain trapped until a period of drought lowers the volume of the river. Because some ledges and falls produce the same effects as dams, they should be considered extremely dangerous until proven otherwise.

Many of the new guide books rate rapids according to the AWA (American White-Water Affiliation) International River Rating Scale. This is most handy, as it allows you to plan a trip with confidence. In guide books where this rating scale has not been followed, you must rely on the individual judgment of the writer, which may be considerably different from your own. The International River Rating Scale is the great equalizer.

AWA INTERNATIONAL RIVER RATING SCALE

Water Class and Characteristics

I. EASY—Bends without difficulty, small rapids with waves regular and low. Obstacles like fallen trees, bridge pilings, and so on. River speed less than hard back-paddling speed.

II. MEDIUM—Fairly frequent but unobstructed rapids with regular waves and low ledges. River speed occasionally exceeding hard back-paddling speed.

III. DIFFICULT—Small falls; large, regular waves covering boat. Expert maneuvering required. Course not always easily recognizable. Current speed usually less than fast forward-paddling speed. (Splash cover useful.)

IV. VERY DIFFICULT—High, powerful waves and difficult eddies. Abrupt bends and difficult broken water. Powerful and precise maneuvering mandatory. (Splash cover essential.)

V. EXCEEDINGLY DIFFICULT—Very fast eddies, violent current, steep drops.

VI. LIMIT OF NAVIGABILITY—Navigable only at select water conditions by teams of experts. Cannot be attempted without risk of life.

Several years ago I drove for many hours to Wisconsin's Flambeau River to run a section of Class III rapids. Despite the fact that water levels were high, the rapid really rated only a class II on the AWA Rating Scale. I learned later that the guide book I had consulted rated all rapids one step above their official AWA difficulty ratings. Of course I enjoyed the run, but I had come for the white-water excitement, which, on this stretch of the river, just wasn't there.

For all practical purposes a loaded wilderness canoe should not be taken into rapids of a higher classification than II. The risks are just too great. You should realize that a heavy spring rain can turn mild Class I rapids into wild IIs or IIIs, and an early fall drought can tame a III to where you can walk right down the middle of it. Water levels are extremely important in sizing up rapids. Where gauging stations exist, interpretive information can be secured from the administrative unit responsible for the gauge. This is usually the U.S. Army Corps of Engineers, the U.S. Weather Bureau, or your state's department of natural resources or conservation.

Your most accurate information, however, will be available from local canoe clubs which maintain their own gauges. These can be anything from a paint mark on a bridge piling to a rusted pipe. Primitive though they are, club gauges reflect the needs of canoeists and hence are most useful.

LINING AND TRACKING

One morning, after some two hours of leisurely paddling down Ontario's Moose River, my partner suddenly realized that he had left his three-hundred-dollar camera at our last campsite. Somewhat begrudgingly and with unrepeatable expletives, I grabbed a painter and helped him tow the canoe seven miles upstream to our island campsite of the night before. I doubt that we could have paddled that distance very easily.

Upstream tracking is not only useful for retrieving lost cameras, but also for getting around rapids when a portage is difficult or impossible to make. For best results while tracking, the upstream end of the canoe should be kept up. If your towing link or ring is located very far above the water line, you will have to disconnect the bow rope and rig a towing harness. You want the line pulling right from the keel, if possible. The stern line is less important and can remain at its usual place of attachment.

Upstream tracking is just like ferrying. By keeping the canoe at a slight angle to the current (bow out, stern toward shore) while towing, you can walk upstream along the bank and the wash of the current will carry the canoe out to the center of the river. Changing the angle of the canoe while pulling on the ropes will return it to shore. Obviously, tracking is impossible if shorelines are too brushy or rugged to walk along.

The opposite of tracking is lining. This procedure is considerably more common than upstream work and is widely used to get around small falls, ledges, and other obstacles in the river. Some authorities recommend attaching lines to keep the upstream end of the canoe raised. They also advise attaching the bow line to a gunwale near the seat. I have found it best to leave lines attached to their customary rings at the bow and stern (which should be located close to the water line). Often, while lining, you will be working above the canoe or, possibly, hopping from rock to rock, sometimes pulling from different sides of the canoe. If, for example, you let the canoe down a chute and for some reason need to pull it back up to realign it with the main current, you will be at a serious disadvantage if your lines are attached anywhere other than at the ends.

You can almost always portage instead of line, and this is considerably safer—although, of course, it is more work. On some arctic rivers where impassable rapids continue for many miles, you may have to line. In the continental United States most river banks are too cluttered with debris to permit lining for any great distance.

WHITE-WATER SAFETY

Despite some dangers inherent in the sport of canoeing, it is essentially a safe pastime. White-water clubs take to the rivers as soon as the ice melts, and although the water temperature is very cold (sometimes just a few degrees above freezing), we seldom hear of a drowning. This is because experienced paddlers respect the rivers and are well prepared for upsets. Herein lies the key to white-water safety: *be prepared for an upset!*

LIFE JACKETS

Many beginners assume that being a good swimmer is the most important safety consideration. While swimming ability is important, a life jacket and a cool head are more important. Except in unusually calm conditions, you should wear your life jacket at all times. On a wilderness trip, especially, you are burdened with the extra weight of heavy clothes and boots. An upset in even a moderate rapid or mildly choppy lake can be hazardous. Lack of a life preserver has accompanied almost every canoeing fatality.

In 1974 a canoeist lost his life on the Coppermine River in the Northwest Territories of Canada. The man was a good swimmer and an experienced white-water paddler. He and his partner put ashore just above a difficult rapid known as Rocky Defile. After considerable scouting the pair decided to run the rapid. As soon as they started downstream, the canoeist realized that he was not wearing his life jacket. He had taken it off while checking the rapid and had neglected to put it back on. But it was too late. The canoe nosed into a heavy roller and began to climb. When it reached the top of the large wave, it teetered and flipped over on its side, throwing both paddlers out of the canoe. Four weeks later the body of the unfortunate canoeist was found. His partner, who wore a life jacket, survived and completed the remaining two hundred miles of the journey alone. It is ironic that in the many miles these experts had paddled together, this was the first time that either had neglected to wear his life jacket. It was not incompetence that cost the life of this canoeist. Rather, it was an oversight—a simple procedural omission—like forgetting to buckle up your seat belt before you drive. Wilderness rivers bear no malice toward unprepared paddlers; neither, however, do they grant immunity from error.

Because your life jacket is so important, you should select a model that you can wear comfortably all the time. Eliminate from consideration the orange horse-collar type; they are too confining and chafe the neck badly. Expect to pay at least twenty-five dollars for a good American or

FIGURE 31a. A few manufacturers are now providing very good Coast Guard–approved life jackets that meet white-water requirements. This *Deliverance* jacket, made by Stearns Manufacturing Company, is ideal for the serious canoeist. (*Photo courtesy of Stearns Manufacturing Co.*)

FIGURE 31b. The safest life jacket is the one you are most likely to keep on. This Gatsby canoe-kayak vest by Stearns is sleek, tough, and comfortable and has over-the-shoulder padding for more comfortable portaging. (*Photo courtesy of Stearns Manufacturing Co.*)

European vest preserver, and don't choose a jacket on the strength of Coast Guard approval tags alone. The life jacket requirements of white-water paddlers are not the same as those of powerboaters. For example, the proper procedure for swimming in rapids is as follows: lie on your back, feet pointing downstream; keep your feet high to prevent somersaulting in the current, and use your feet and canoe paddle to ward off rocks; swim on your back or side, at an angle to the current, to reach shore. This technique is similar to the canoeist's back ferry.

To do this you need as much flotation on your back as on your chest, and the bulky horse collars offer virtually no back flotation. Horse collars are designed to float the wearer head up for extended periods of time, at the expense of maneuverability. You are seldom in the water for more than five minutes in a typical canoe upset. In order to avoid obstacles you need a jacket that does not interfere with swimming. This should be a major consideration. Fortunately, the Coast Guard is beginning to realize that the needs of canoeists are best met with a specialized type of jacket. Consequently, some of the best life jackets, which a few years ago were outlawed, are now receiving Coast Guard approval. The safest life jacket is the one the canoeist is most likely to keep wearing, and this is usually the one that is most comfortable. Buy the *best* jacket available, even if the cost seems prohibitive. Your life is too precious to skimp here.

It is interesting to note that there is little relationship between your weight out of water and your weight in water. Prospective buyers of life jackets assume that a 250-pound man needs more flotation than a 130-pound teenager. If the man is overweight and the teenager is mostly muscle, quite the opposite may be true. It is not uncommon for children to need as much flotation as their parents. Manufacturers have done an excellent job providing properly sized life jackets. The important thing, however, is to realize that the buoyancy rating of the jacket may or may not meet your requirements. You should test your life jacket in both calm water and rapids to assure that it will adequately support you.

KEEPING WARM

Almost all white-water canoeists wear wet suits for protection from cold water in the early spring. Wet suits are bulky to pack and are hot and uncomfortable to wear. For these reasons they are seldom carried on wilderness trips, although they are beginning to show up. If you know you will be running difficult rapids in very cold water, a wet suit, or at least a neoprene vest, should be included in your equipment.

Most modern canoeists still rely on wool for warmth. Wool is the best material for keeping you warm when you are wet (Polyester Fiberfill II and Polar Guard are also good in this respect). Wear at least two layers of wool next to your skin. Before venturing down difficult rapids in the cold water of early spring, I usually don a waterproof paddling shirt under my life jacket. The shirt fits tightly at the neck, waist, and sleeves, provides great warmth for its weight, and considerably reduces the possibility of getting chilled both in and out of the water.

As the table below shows, your body will remain functional in cold water for only a short time. Even this doesn't tell the whole story, because the initial shock of the cold water on your chest saps much of your energy. A paddling shirt can reduce this shock somewhat, but only a wet suit can eliminate it completely.

WATER TEMPERATURE	AMOUNT OF TIME BODY WILL REMAIN FUNCTIONAL
less than 40 degrees	less than 10 minutes
40–50 degrees	15 20 minutes
50–60 degrees	15–40 minutes
60 degrees and above	one or more hours

Although your body may remain functional for several minutes in cold water, you can die from hypothermia after you have been rescued. Hypothermia occurs when body temperature drops below ninety-five degrees Fahrenheit. As blood is rushed to the vital organs, chilling spreads throughout the body. This is accompanied by clumsiness, slurred speech, and loss of judgment. Coma and death may occur within a few hours if body temperature is not raised. Should a member of your party experience hypothermia, *immediately* place him or her near a fire or into a sleeping bag with a person of normal temperature. Administer hot liquids and small amounts of food with salt.

In 1974 an expedition down the Kaniapiskau River in northern Quebec province experienced several days of very cold driving rain. When the paddlers put ashore at the end of a particularly arduous day, they were cold, wet, and very tired. It was evident to the trip leader that immediate action was necessary to prevent hypothermia. An attempt was made to start the gasoline stove to prepare tea, but it refused to function. There was no backup stove. Since the expedition was above the tree line, there was little available wood, and that which could be found was too wet to burn. In a desperate effort to provide heat, the party chopped up an expensive canoe paddle to supply fuel for a warming fire and avoided the serious possibility of hypothermia, thanks to the quick thinking of the expedition leader.

BASIC PRECAUTIONS

When you are canoeing white water, avoid long coats, ponchos, or anything dangling around your neck on a string. Should you overturn, these items are likely to be caught on submerged tree limbs or between rocks. Also avoid heavy boots, and *never* wear waders while paddling. Water-filled waders can make swimming in even a moderate current impossible.

If you overturn your best life preserver is the canoe, and you should stay with it unless doing so will endanger your life. If you have water-proofed your gear and outfitted your canoe with rubber ropes as recommended, the additional flotation of your packs will keep your canoe floating high. Since white water is mostly air, you will have difficulty breathing, even with a good life jacket. A high-riding canoe will keep you above the foamy water.

Upon upsetting, swim immediately to the *upstream* end of the canoe. A water-filled canoe weighs more than a ton, and should you get between it and a rock you will be crushed. Hang onto the grab loop or stern painter and try to swim the canoe to shore. The canoe-over-canoe rescue touted by the Red Cross and Scouts works well on calm lakes with *empty* canoes, but cannot be done with loaded canoes on fast water. Unfortunately, this is where most canoe upsets occur.

7.
Canoe Salvage and Repair

SALVAGE

If your canoe overturns in a difficult rapid and spins broadside to the current, it may be forcefully dashed against a rock or swept under a submerged tree or brush pile. Here the craft may remain firmly wedged until ingenuity or low water sets it free. And when you're three hundred miles from the nearest road, you have no choice. Some canoeists carry a small block and tackle for such emergencies, but you can rig a multiple pulley with a power cinch (see Chapter 9—Tying It All Together) by taking several loops on the haul back line. On difficult trips I usually carry a couple of *carabiners* (aluminum fittings through which mountain climbers run their ropes) and a compact nylon pulley. The caribiners and pulley reduce rope friction considerably. If you have one hundred or more feet of rope (which you should have on a wilderness trip), you can rig a two to one mechanical advantage (or greater) pulley over a short distance. If the canoe is really hung up badly, even this may not be enough. However, if you rig a harness around the canoe and experiment (don't attach to fittings—you'll pull them loose), you can usually jockey the hull around into a position that will reduce the water pressure against it. With some effort, thought, extreme patience, and much muscle power, you can usually find a way to get the canoe free. If the canoe is well submerged or wrapped around an obstacle so tightly that your best efforts won't get it loose, at least wait around for a few days before abandoning it. Rivers often fluctuate greatly from week to week, and an inch or two less water may provide just the edge you need to work your canoe free.

In canoeing, two pounds of prevention is more valuable than a half-ounce of cure, and when you realize that even a slow-moving, peaceful river can power a giant mill wheel, you begin to gain an appreciation of the power of moving water.

If your canoe should ground firmly upon a rock in a fast-flowing river and turn broadside to the current, the entire side of the craft will be exposed to the force of the rushing water. This force may equal several thousand pounds, and may be enough to bend or break a fragile canoe. However, as long as the craft is kept upright, the rushing water will usually pass harmlessly beneath the rounded hull. But if the upstream gunwale should dip below the water and expose the inside of the canoe to the power of the current, the water's force will not be dissipated. A canoe in this position may be severely damaged. It may even be broken in half, or if it's aluminum, be wrapped tightly around the rock. Therefore it is important that you *never* let the open end of your craft become exposed to the current. You should make every effort to keep the upstream gunwale up, even if it means leaving your canoe. If necessary, jump into the water on the *upstream* side of the canoe. Hold tightly to the gunwale and try to work the canoe loose. Usually the removal of your weight is all that is necessary to free the hull. Do not, however, under *any* circumstances, enter the water *downstream* of the canoe. Should the craft slide off the rock while you are in the water, it could crush you against a downstream obstacle.

REPAIR

Modern canoeists use silver duct (furnace) tape almost exclusively for field repairs of canoes. Duct tape sticks—to anything! In fact, canoe owners often neglect more permanent hull repairs simply because furnace tape works so well. A small roll of duct tape should be carried on *all* canoe trips—close to home or otherwise. In twenty-five years of canoeing I have yet to damage a canoe so badly that tape and ingenuity would not repair it.

In the case of aluminum canoes, there is little you can do in the way of field repairs other than apply tape. Where rivets have been pulled they can be retightened by administering several blows with the back side of an ax. Small gaps and holes can be filled with liquid aluminum or epoxy, and these items should be included in your repair kit. Since aluminum canoes usually bend rather than break, physical force will be required to straighten them. An aluminum canoe that has had its gunwales or sides caved in can be placed in shallow water, sand, or mud and stomped back into a semblance of shape. A wood block, the hammer face of an ax, and true grit will produce amazing results. At home a break in the skin should be repaired by affixing a riveted patch. Complete patch kits, available from the Grumman Corporation, include patching material, rivets, and instructions. Although a good-quality welding job appears to hold satisfactorily, the aluminum adjacent to the weld may become brittle and cause problems later on. I have seen some fine repair jobs by master aircraft aluminum welders, and these are probably adequate.

One canoe owned by a very skilled white-water paddler has been lovingly named *Super Beater*. This ancient Grumman canoe was broken completely in half in a Class III rapid and welded back together. The gunwales have been welded in perhaps a dozen places, and the keel was ripped off and a shoe keel fused in its place. *Super Beater* seems to perform unusually well in heavy rapids, despite its appearance. Its owner remains totally oblivious to the possibility of any future damage.

Fiberglass, Kevlar, and cedar strip canoes are easily repaired by applying epoxy resin and fiberglass cloth directly to the break. You can substitute polyester resin for epoxy, but it isn't nearly as strong.* Epoxy resin in quart or larger quantities is not readily available in all parts of the country. If you have difficulty locating a supply, you can order it directly from the Sears catalogue. For a perfect color match, COLOR AGENT tubes are available almost everywhere.

ABS Royalex hulls are so tough that they are nearly puncture-

* Unfortunately, the hardening speed of epoxy is dependent upon temperature and humidity. It may take several days for epoxy to cure if the weather is cold and damp. Polyester, on the other hand, if given an overdose of MEK Peroxide hardener, will set up in a few hours. Use epoxy for home repairs and polyester for trips.

proof. Although I did own a Royalex canoe once, I confess to no first-hand experience in repairing this material. A special patching compound, available from the Old Town Canoe Company, is said to do an excellent job. Write to Old Town for details (see Appendix C for further information).

If you own a fine wood-canvas canoe, you are probably well aware of how to maintain it. Both the Chestnut and Old Town canoe companies offer everything you need for complete restoration of one of these craft. Wood-canvas canoes never die; they just accumulate new parts. For detailed instructions on how to repair wood-canvas canoes, consult the American Red Cross's canoeing manual; it provides a wealth of information on the subject.

8.
Tripping with Tots and Teens

TRIPPING WITH TOTS

On her second birthday my daughter Clarissa received a pretty blue Stearn's life jacket, and on her third birthday a miniature laminated canoe paddle. Peggy Ann, a year behind Clarissa, followed suit, and when Santa popped through the ventilator last December, both girls discovered, carefully wrapped under the Christmas tree, yearling-size sleeping bags, down-filled and covered with powder blue nylon taffeta.

The preschool years generally mean trading in the canoe and camping gear for a super-size color TV and stereo. However, this need not be the case. There is a way to enjoy both canoeing and your children—and that way is to take a family canoe trip.

Before committing yourself to a canoe trip with preschoolers, prepare yourself for an onslaught of disapproving stares, glares, and verbal assaults at any mention of plans for putting little nonswimming Johnny or Jenny into a "tippy" canoe. Your qualifications as a parent may come under question. Nevertheless, once you are convinced that canoeing with toddlers is safe (and it is if proper precautions are taken), you will be well prepared to deal with the criticism which you are sure to encounter.

GET SOME INSTRUCTION

Although it is seldom mentioned, the greatest safety margin that you can provide for your children is for you to be both a competent swimmer and a reasonably good canoeist. These two factors will keep you out of trouble in almost all situations in which you have non-swimmers aboard. If there is a canoe club nearby, join it. If not, read and reread the good books on canoeing available in your local library. Then, get out and practice—without the kids. At any rate, do join your state canoe association. If you don't know its address, your state's department of natural resources has probably worked with the canoe association from time to time and should be able to tell you how to contact it. As a member of a canoe club, you will become acquainted with other canoeing families, and your mind will be more at ease knowing there are others to share your experiences and help with problems.

KIDS ARE LITTLE PEOPLE

Perhaps the most important thing to remember about toddlers is that they are little people. I have seen parents set their children down in the middle of a canoe with only a life jacket. Without adequate insulation under them, a comfortable backrest, or a place to sleep protected from wind and sun, preschoolers quickly show their dissatisfaction by crying, screaming, and kicking, none of which tends to enhance the quietude of the wilderness setting. These undesirable responses may be reduced, if not eliminated entirely, by making your little ones as comfortable as possible and by making sure you have the proper equipment.

THE PROPER EQUIPMENT

First and foremost is the life jacket. Toddlers absolutely must wear their life jackets at all times. A bit of psychology helps—and generally this means that both mom and dad set an example. Since the rocking motion of a canoe is conducive to extra-long naps, it is important that the life jackets your children wear be extremely comfortable ones that they can sleep in. The $3.98 kapok models are excellent in case of an upset, as they float the child's head well out of the water, but they are very uncomfortable and should be avoided if at all possible.

Stearn's of Minnesota makes several models suitable for preschoolers, including a unique doughnut-shaped life preserver called the Kindergåård®. Stearn's jackets are comfortable, stylish, and float the head high. Although expensive, they are an excellent investment for the safety of your child, since children will wear them happily even through their naps. Swim-aids, while more attractive and less expensive than Coast Guard–approved life jackets, should be avoided, for they will not keep the head of a nonswimmer afloat.

The bottom of a canoe (aluminum models, at least) may run only a few degrees warmer than the temperature of the water. Consequently it is important to cover the bottom with adequate cushioning for both insulation and comfort. The best solution is to place an air mattress, nylon-covered foam pad, or piece of Ensolite foam on the bottom of the canoe for the children to sit on and later to curl up on for a nap. Children will want to sit up and view the countryside, so a backrest of some kind should be provided. A foam cushion makes a suitable backrest when propped up against a canoe thwart, and when nap time rolls around it makes a good pillow as well.

Each child should have his or her favorite blanket and toy. By all means provide a canoe paddle of miniature dimensions, for children love to paddle (it is wise to tie a string to the paddle and to secure this string to a canoe thwart). Don't become disenchanted by your passenger's inability to paddle properly. Let kids play with their paddles as they wish (just so they don't hit each other, or you), for this is part of their good time.

A complete change of clothes from nose to toes must be provided, and rain gear is very important. The best rain covering for toddlers is a poncho. The hood and extra-long body of the poncho will cover a child completely. A less expensive solution is to provide each child with a plastic leaf-and-lawn-size garbage bag. Merely cut a slit for the head in the top of the bag and furnish a "souwester" style hat to go with it.

It is also advisable to bring along a spare blanket. When children fall asleep in the canoe, they may need additional insulation not provided by their security blankets. Lastly, a lightweight nylon or Visqueen plastic fly of about eight by ten feet is desirable for shelter in case you want to get off the water during a heavy rain, or as a cover for the kids when they are sleeping, should a light rain begin.

FIGURE 32. Finding a suitable life preserver for the baby of the family is a problem. This Kindergåård® Infant Life Vest is a brand-new development from Stearns Manufacturing Company. The life jacket is Coast Guard–approved for all boating activities.

Note: This is the *only* comfortable life jacket currently available for toddlers. The jacket is easy to get on and off and is streamlined in the chest area to allow for the baby's use of hands and arms.

In addition to food and drink for the day, bring a thermos of milk for the kids and some penny candy. Plan to stop for a few minutes each hour, and allow time for fun and games during the lunch break. Generally, river trips of about ten miles are ideal; longer trips tend to get somewhat trying for both children and adults, and three or four hours on the water is plenty with young children. For toddlers in diapers, the disposable kind are indispensible. Take several, packed in a waterproof plastic bag, and place used diapers in a plastic bag to be brought home for proper disposal.

All clothing, food, and equipment must be adequately waterproofed. An easy and inexpensive way to do this is to place everything in a plastic trash can. Carefully seal the lid of the trash can with silver duct tape. The tape seal can be removed and resealed often without losing its effectiveness, and the rigid plastic container will protect crushables.

It should go without saying that river sections with rapids should be avoided—even by highly skilled canoeists. Very mild, bouncing water can, of course, be paddled and adds to the fun. Such "rapids" are generally shallow enough to walk through. A final word of safety: if you have two nonswimmers aboard, decide before the trip how you will handle an upset should it occur. Generally one parent goes after each child. *Do not* take three nonswimmers on a canoe trip when there are only two swimmers to watch them. Should you overturn, your first responsibility is to your children. With everyone wearing life jackets in a slow-moving river or placid lake, rescue should present no problems, especially if another canoe is nearby.

I must admit that my wife and I have never overturned our canoe with young children aboard, but we have helped rescue other families who have. When the initial displeasure is followed by warm clothes, a roaring fire, and hot chocolate, even the crankiest child is ready for more. A family canoe trip brings the kind of warmth and well-being which too many of us have forgotten in this age of electronic gratification.

TRIPPING WITH TEENS

For the most part, tripping with teenagers is a rewarding and relaxing experience—provided, of course, that the trip is properly planned and the group is not too large. Over the past twenty years I have organized and participated in at least fifty different canoe trips with

young people. Trips have varied in length from one to fifteen days, and
groups have ranged in size from two to thirty persons. I have reached
the conclusion that to minimize environmental damage (and preserve
your sanity), you should limit the group to ten people—including two
adults. Should an emergency arise and a youngster need to be returned
quickly to civilization, one can go with the evacuee, and one can stay
with the group.

Where sufficient adult leaders cannot be found, a party of sixteen
teenagers can be split into two groups of eight and accompanied by one
adult each. If the two groups stay within close proximity of each other
during the trip, both adults will be available should a crisis develop.

Kids are pretty honest with adults. If they don't like something,
they'll tell you right off. It may be the food, the rain, the ruggedness of
the trip, or the way you are running things that they find fault with.
And youngsters are often right—from their point of view. This is an
important consideration, for if you are tripping with teenagers you are
doing so for *their* benefit, not yours. In planning a trip, remember that
youngsters lack your experience and maturity. Their kind of trip may
not necessarily be your kind of trip. If they are beginners they will have
difficulty accepting uncomfortable conditions resulting from bad weather
or poor planning.

Trip planning is your responsibility, and each youngster should be
provided with a complete checklist of what to bring. In addition, you may
have to hold a full field inspection. Teenagers will almost always forget
something, unless they are very conscientious. Usually they forget minor
things like a toothbrush or comb, but occasionally they will omit something more important, like boots or rain gear. Another reason for an
equipment inspection is that teenagers don't realize that good equipment
is essential to their comfort. To them a sleeping bag is a sleeping bag,
and girls, especially, will show up with $8.95 slumber bags unless you
check their sleeping gear. This often isn't the fault of the youngster,
whose parents don't always understand that all sleeping bags are not
equally warm.

Rain gear is always a problem. To save money parents will usually
buy their children cheap plastic ponchos or rain suits which won't hold
up for more than a day or two in rough weather. This type of rain gear
may be adequate for an especially dry time of year, but if you expect
rain the youngsters and their parents should know that reliable, good-
quality rain cover will be necessary.

Regardless of the intellectual ability of the kids, you will have to deal with one frustrating and almost universal teenage problem—carelessness. Young people are unbelievably careless, even with their own equipment. I have seen teenagers who should know better throw expensive down sleeping bags into the wet bottom of a canoe, or lay them out in muddy grass or too near a fire. Unthinking teenagers leave food lying around which attracts animals, and they procrastinate dishwashing well into the night. They almost never remember to remove drying clothing from clotheslines before they retire, and in spite of stern warnings to the contrary they burn up at least one boot or pair of socks in the campfire while attempting to dry them. Their sanitary habits are usually completely undeveloped. If no latrine is available, they just go in the woods. They wash their hair, bodies, and dishes in the river or lake with little concern for possible water contamination, and less than ten minutes later they draw water for drinking from the same spot.

With proper planning most of these pitfalls can be avoided. Young people should be shown how to dispose of garbage, construct latrines, and clean up an area properly *before* the trip, not while it is in progress. Environmental etiquette should be stressed throughout the wilderness experience. For example, I commonly tell girls and boys that hair washing is not permitted within fifty feet of the lake or river. This, I explain, is to prevent water pollution. The kids enjoy doing their part for the environment and soon develop a cooperative method of shampooing, complete with hot water and a bucket brigade.

Unless a group of teenagers has had considerable canoe-camping experience, they are apt to forget items of equipment on the portage trail or when they break camp. The only effective way I've found to deal with this problem is to make each youngster responsible for something. For example, one boy might be responsible for a food pack, the stove, and the cook kit. He should know the exact place of every item in the food pack, and should check at the end of each portage to make sure everything is present. Another member might be responsible for the gas can, ax, and fishing rod case. Youngsters quickly learn the importance of each item of equipment and accept their responsibility without complaint. On the few occasions where an article is left behind, the person responsible for it will usually volunteer to go back after it.

In June 1975 I took seven teenagers on a one-week trip into Minnesota's Boundary Waters Canoe Area. It happened that another teen group had selected the same route as ours, and for three days we trailed

about an hour behind them. At the end of the three days we had accumulated two canoe paddles, one rain jacket, one sweatshirt, a pair of sunglasses, a bottle of insect repellent, and one gallon of gasoline (for their
stove). When we finally caught up we were able to effect a trade of needed
items. We swapped their lost equipment for two pounds of popcorn and
some margarine. We were all well satisfied with the exchange.

A very necessary item when tripping with teenagers is a well-filled
first-aid kit. Make especially sure you have plenty of Band-Aids. Most
injuries are minor and occur while whittling or swimming. Carry at
least three Band-Aids per group member—on one canoe trip I used
eighteen Band-Aids for seven kids.

A controversial item is the ax. I am in disagreement with authorities who suggest bringing along a large, long-handled ax. I carry only a
quality-built, all-steel hand ax and I do *not* allow youngsters to use it for
chopping. All wood is cut with a small folding saw; the ax is used only
for splitting it. I permit only one method of splitting: the hand ax is
driven into the upright log with just enough force to hold it in place;
the splitter then uses both hands to grasp the handle firmly; a second
person uses a 16-inch length of 4- to 6-inch diameter log to hammer the
ax head through the log to be split. This method necessarily requires
two people: one to hold the ax, and the other to hammer. Because the
ax is all steel, no damage to the handle can result. But most important,
there is no danger of cut toes, knees, or thighs. You don't have enough
time on the average canoe trip to show youngsters how to use an ax
properly, and regardless of the quality of instruction on your part, most
beginners cannot develop sufficient skill in a day or two to be reliably
ax-competent.

I agree with authorities who urge you to avoid the ¾ Hudson Bay,
or short ax; its short handle makes it a very dangerous tool. A full-
length ax, on the other hand, is just extra weight in this day of small fires
and fuel conservation. Regardless of the ax you select, the handle just
back of the head should be made of steel, or reinforced with fiberglass if
it is wood. Teenagers are very adept at breaking ax handles.

I have found it best to go slow and easy the first day of a canoe trip,
and to pick up the speed on the second day. Stop early enough each day
to allow plenty of time for play and fishing. Include at least one day that
is a real challenge, begin at dawn that day and camp at sunset. Paddle
hard, and, where they are available, select rugged portages. Such a day

is necessary to mold the group into oneness. Plan to spend a full day in camp after your rugged day.

A teen group which I tripped with in August 1975 was extremely slow, both in paddling and on the portages. Where other groups of similar age would complete a portage in forty-five minutes, they would take ninety. I jokingly nicknamed them "my sweet pokeys." Then one night while we were sitting around the campfire, I asked to read their diaries (I require that each individual keep a diary). I found that most had written beautiful, poetic things about the trees, the lakes, and the beauty of nature. With this came a realization. Unlike faster groups, my sweet pokeys had gained a respect and appreciation for the wilderness. They had developed the exact attitudes that I was trying to instill. Instead of rushing through the wilderness, they were looking at it. I was ashamed that I had mocked them, and I apologized for my thought-lessness.

9.
Tying It All Together

Every canoeist should have a fundamental knowledge of knot-tying and rope-handling techniques. You will use ropes for lining and tracking your canoe through rapids, hauling food up a tree to keep it away from animals, erecting a rain tarp, making a clothesline, lifting a bucket of cold water from the depths of a lake, securing your canoe to a car-top carrier, salvage and rescue operations, and many other purposes.

Many outdoors handbooks define a dozen or more knots. In reality, unless you are a mountain climber or intend to chop down the forest to build rope-lashed furniture (which isn't even remotely humorous in this age of environmental awareness), you can get along very nicely with just two hitches and two knots. These are the *double half-hitch* (two *half-hitches*), *sheet bend, bowline,* and *power-cinch*. Those familiar with rope-handling techniques will note the conspicuous absence of the square knot and the tautline hitch. Except for limited first-aid applications the square knot is generally useless, and the much touted tautline hitch has gone the way of the passenger pigeon. The tautline was useful in the days of cotton tents and manila rope; it has been replaced with the much handier, more versatile, power-cinch.

Admittedly, I find that most canoeists can usually get by with just one knot and one hitch—the power-cinch and the sheet bend. These are a must, however, and they should be mastered before you undertake a voyage of significance.

THE DOUBLE HALF-HITCH
(*two half-hitches*)

The double half-hitch is useful for tying a rope to a tree or to the towing link of a canoe. The knot is very secure and tends to tighten itself when a load is applied to the rope.

THE SHEET BEND

Use the sheet bend for tying two ropes together. The knot works well even if the rope sizes differ greatly. The sheet bend is about the only knot that can be effectively used to join the ends of slippery polypropylene rope.

A friend of mine won five dollars when he fixed a broken waterskiing tow-rope with this knot. When the tow-line snapped, the owner of the ski boat bet my friend that he couldn't tie the two ends of the polypropylene rope back together tightly enough to hold. My friend won the bet and skied the remainder of the day on the repaired line.

It is important that the free ends of the sheet bend be on the *same side,* as shown in figure 33. The knot will work if the ends are on opposite sides, but will be less reliable. Use the sheet bend for joining your fifty-foot nylon line to your twenty-foot polypropylene painter.

THE BOWLINE

The bowline is a very secure knot which won't slip, regardless of the load applied. It is commonly used by mountain climbers to tie their climbing ropes around their waists. Use this knot whenever you want to put a nonslip loop on the end of a line.

Beginners are often told to make the bowline by forming a loop, or "rabbit hole." The rabbit (free end of the rope) comes up through the

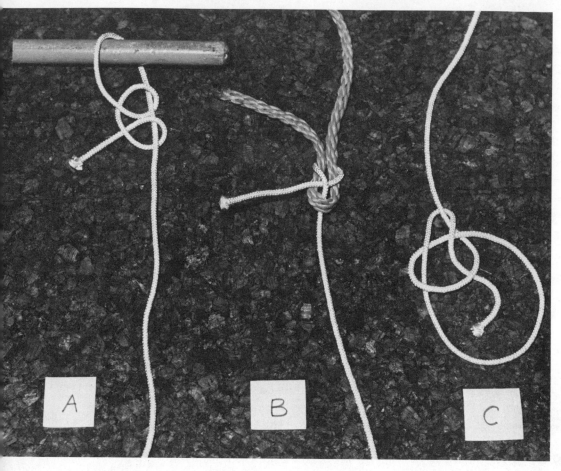

FIGURE 33. a. Two half hitches b. Sheet bend c. Bowline

hole, around the tree (opposite or long end of the rope shown in figure 33c) and back down the hole. The bowline will slip a few inches before it tightens, so allow an extra-long free end.

THE POWER-CINCH

Perhaps the most ingenious hitch to come along in recent years is the power-cinch (there seems to be no widely accepted name for this hitch; hence, I took the liberty of naming it the "power-cinch"), which effectively replaces the tautline hitch and functions as a powerful pulley when used properly. Skilled canoeists use this pulley knot almost exclu-

sively for tying canoes on cars. It is also widely used by truckers who
tie heavy loads in place. The power-cinch may be the canoeist's most
useful hitch.

Begin the power-cinch by forming the loop shown in figure 34,
step 1. Pull the loop through as in step 2. It is important that the loop
be formed *exactly* as shown. The loop will look okay if you make it back-
wards, but it won't work.

If the loop is formed as in step 2, a simple tug on the rope will
eliminate it. This is preferable to the common practice of tying a knot
in the loop, which, after being exposed to a load, is almost impossible
to get out.

If you are tying a canoe into place on top of a car, tie one end of the
rope to the canoe's bow or stern and snap the steel hook on the other end

FIGURE 34. *The Versatile Power-Cinch* (Steps in tying)

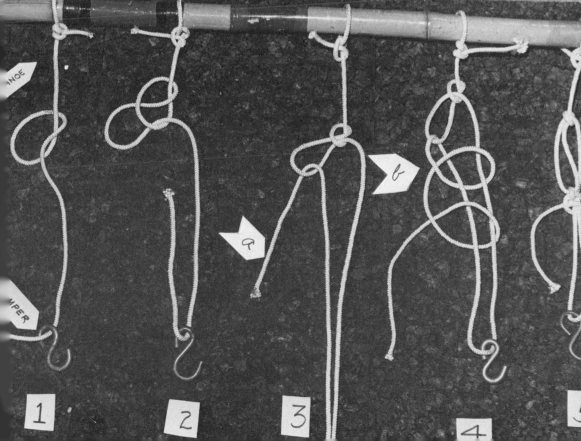

of the rope to the car's bumper. Run the free end of the rope (a) through the loop in step 3. Now apply power to the free end. You have, in effect, created a pulley with a two-to-one mechanical advantage. The power you can get out of this system has to be seen to be believed; if it is used to secure the bow or stern of a car-topped canoe to a car bumper, you can, if you are careless, actually pull the rope hard enough to break the back of a wood canoe or seriously bend an aluminum model. You can pull a clothesline tight enough to cause it to sing like a taut guitar string when plucked with the fingers.

Complete the hitch by securing a double half-hitch around the body of the rope, as in step 4. Tighten the half-hitches (step 5) to complete the knot.

For additional power, which is needed, for example, in canoe salvage operations, you can form several loops in the rope body like the ones shown in step 2. The more loops, the greater the mechanical advantage and the more power you can exert. When you form additional loops, however, it is important that each pulley be completed separately. For example, to form an additional pulley in step 3, the loop would be formed in that part of the line closest to the number 3 (the left rope—not the right one). Once you learn to form the basic knot, the principal of adding loops will become evident.

The power-cinch is ideal for securing gear in canoes, especially if the knot is completed with a single quick-release half-hitch. Make the quick-release feature by forming one half-hitch as shown in step 4b. Then pull the free end of the rope partway back through the loop at b and tighten the hitch. This is exactly like tying your shoes with a quick-release bow. A pull on the free end of the rope will release the hitch.

SECURING A LINE

On a wilderness trip several years ago one canoe of our party swamped in a heavy rapid. There was a bouldery falls about two hundred yards downstream, and it was imperative that we get a rope to the wet canoeists immediately in order to avoid disaster. Luckily, a fifty-foot line was at hand and was properly coiled for throwing. The line was heaved to the two men who were hanging onto the gunwales of the water-filled canoe. Fortunately the men caught the rope, and both they and the canoe were pulled safely to shore, avoiding what might have been a serious mishap.

You should always keep your ropes coiled and ready for use. The best system I have found is an old Navy method:

1. Coil the rope around your arm, grasp the main body of it with one hand, and place your thumb through the eye of the coils to hold them in place, as shown in figure 35a.

2. Remove the last two coils of rope, take this long free end, and wind it around the main body of the rope several times (figure 35b). Wind the free end *downward*, toward the hand holding the rope body. Wind evenly and snugly. Don't make the coils too tight.

FIGURE 35a. *Securing a Line.* Step 1.   FIGURE 35b. Step 2.

FIGURE 35c. Step 3.   FIGURE 35d. Step 4.

3. Form a loop with the free end of the rope, as shown in figure 35c, and push it through the eye of the rope body.

4. Grasp the wound coils with one hand and the rope body with the other hand and slide the coils upward tightly against the loop. The rope is now coiled and secured (figure 35d). Pulling the free end of the rope will release the line, which can quickly be made ready for throwing.

For safety's sake I keep my fifty-foot painters secured in this manner and tucked under a deck-mounted shock cord. This keeps them from snagging in their own coils, yet permits instant accessibility. Throwing-lines secured by this method can be tied around a thwart (merely run the free end of the rope around the thwart and through the loop protruding from the rope's eye. Tie with a quick-release half-hitch). Should you overturn, you won't lose your rope, and it will be quickly and easily available if it is needed.

10.
The
Necessities

It's commonplace to walk through the aisles of a modern camping store and see shelf after shelf of specialized backpacking equipment. Lightweight mountain tents, boots with Vibram-lugged soles, miniature gasoline stoves, and brightly colored down-filled parkas are but a few of the offerings designed especially for the self-sufficient hiker. More often than not, equipment which is suitable for backpacking is also well adapted to canoe camping—but not always. In their rush to the equipment shops, many paddlers forget the essential fact that canoeing is not backpacking. Wading in knee-deep water for hours at a time or sloshing through a mucky, mosquito-infested swamp is very unlike walking down a windswept mountain trail. When selecting equipment, consider how it will perform when soaked with water or covered with sand and mud. These are some of the realities that determine its suitability for wilderness canoe tripping.

PACKS AND SUBSTITUTES

FRAMELESS PACKS

For short, close-to-home trips you don't need expensive pack sacks. You can make do very nicely with inexpensive duffel bags. Line duffel bags with one or two heavy plastic sacks before inserting your belongings; this will make them completely waterproof. Two duffel bags can easily be stuffed under the center thwart of most canoes and still allow plenty of room for two children or an adult passenger.

For short portages you can carry duffel bags "army style" over your shoulder, but for long carries it will be best to rig a tumpline. Make the tumpline by attaching two stout ropes or strips of cotton webbing to a 2-foot length of 3-inch-wide canvas. Tie the ropes or buckle the webbing tightly around the bag. Place the tump strap just above your forehead, lean forward, and take off. Once you get used to it, you can carry moderate loads up to a mile with little difficulty using this system.

If you're planning a trip of a more serious nature, you will want to invest in one or more authentic pack sacks. The most popular, and the best for wilderness canoeing, is the Duluth pack, or "grunt sack," as it is often called. The Duluth pack is a large envelope-style sack made of 15- to 20-ounce per square yard canvas. Straps are usually made of heavy leather and are well secured to the pack with brass rivets and waxed thread. A stout tumpline is sometimes provided. Needless to say, Duluth packs are extremely rugged. They are commonly sized as follows:

Number 2: 24 inches wide by 28 inches deep; weight about 2½ pounds
Number 3: 24 inches wide by 30 inches deep; weight about 3½ pounds
Number 4: 28 inches wide by 30 inches deep, with a 6-inch side wall (set
     out) ; weight about 4 pounds

The number 3 size is the most popular, although some canoeists prefer the larger number 4 for lightweight, bulky items like sleeping bags and clothing.

Even with the tumpline in place, a heavy Duluth pack weighing from sixty-five to eighty-five pounds is not a pleasure to carry. Nevertheless, Duluth packs have been the standard canoe-tripping packs for well over a century, and frankly, nothing better has come along. First of all, grunt sacks are commodious. There are few, if any, frame packs available which can carry the load of a number 3 or 4 Duluth. Second, it is easy to waterproof the contents of these packs by inserting a large plastic bag, or, better, an army waterproof clothes bag (available at low cost from most surplus stores) into them. And last, Duluth packs are designed to sit upright in a canoe instead of on their backs or bellies, like pack sacks of more conventional design.

This stand-up feature is of especial value when you take water in rapids or heavy waves. You can literally fill the canoe with water, and as long as you remain right side up no water can enter the plastic liner of the pack. This is because the weakest part of any waterproof bag is its closure, and this closure is just beneath the flap of the erect Duluth pack—out of contact with accumulated water. This seemingly unimportant design feature became evident to me on a Canadian river trip during which my partner and I repeatedly filled our canoe with water in the heavy rapids we encountered. At no time did we get a single drop of water into any of our food or equipment, although our companions in another canoe had some problems with a specially built, extra-long Duluth pack they were carrying. To keep the canoe's center of gravity low, our friends laid the long pack on its back. In spite of reasonable waterproofing precautions, a small leak developed at the closure of the 10-mil-thick plastic pack liner. That night we resmoked two pounds of damp, homemade deer jerky—though I must admit the smoke was more useful in controlling the black flies than in drying the jerky.

A virtue of Duluth packs that should not be overlooked is the ease with which they fit into the unique contours of a canoe without wasting space, enabling you to pack your gear closely around the yoke to keep the ends of the canoe light for better response in rough water. And because a fully loaded number 2 or 3 Duluth pack only comes a few inches above the gunwales of most canoes (number 4 packs come somewhat higher), the center of gravity of the canoe can be kept low for greater stability. All of which means Duluth packs, especially in the number 2 and 3 sizes, are just about perfect for wilderness canoe tripping.

PACKS WITH FRAMES

Packs with exterior aluminum frames have three major failings when used in canoes: the frames catch on seats, gunwales, and thwarts during loading and unloading operations; the rigid design prevents efficient utilization of space, which can result in a poorly balanced load; and it is difficult to waterproof the contents of the many zippered compartments. Frame outfits, however, are easier to carry, and if you do a considerable amount of backpacking they may be a better investment than the less versatile Duluth packs.

A good method of waterproofing frame packs is to place equipment inside a plastic bag in each pack compartment (envelope-style plastic bags with nylon coil zippers are best). Bring along a few extra zipper bags and plenty of tape—the bags frequently tear. Another solution is to put the pack and frame into a large 10-mil-thick plastic bag, over which a cotton or burlap sack is placed. The sack will prevent the plastic bag from becoming damaged. On portages, merely slide the pack out of its protective cover, roll up the sack and plastic bag, stuff them under the pack flap, and hit the trail.

The best way to use a pack frame (if you must use one) is to remove the pack bag and use the frame by itself. Lay out your tent or nylon tarp and place sleeping bags, foam pads or air mattresses, and clothing in the center. Fold over the edges of the tarp and roll the whole thing up. Tie the roll to your pack frame and shove the ax and saw under the ropes. For two persons, this will result in a total load of about fifty pounds. Such a load can easily be carried short distances by almost anyone, and the package is, of course, absolutely waterproof.

PACK BASKETS

Many canoe-campers line their food packs with shellacked cardboard cartons. The cartons give rigidity to the pack and protect delicate foodstuffs from getting mashed when the pack is thrown into the canoe or onto the ground. A more traditional and better solution to the problem of breakables is the Adirondack pack basket.

For centuries Indians used baskets woven from splints of black ash to carry their belongings. When the white man discovered how handy these baskets were, he adopted them for canoeing. Today some Winnebago and Chippewa groups in northern and central Wisconsin still make baskets, as do the Cherokees in North Carolina. Splint baskets can also be found in a few isolated areas of New England.

Pack baskets have become very popular among New England canoeists while remaining virtually unknown in other canoe areas. Consequently, they are not readily available in most parts of the country. If you want a basket you'll have to order it by mail (the most complete source is L. L. Bean, Inc., Freeport, Maine 04032). Prices are very reasonable considering the amount of hand labor involved.

Pack baskets are sold according to pecks. A three-peck basket stands about eighteen inches high and a four-peck model about twenty-one inches high. You can pack camera, stove, cook kit, thermos, or anything else which might be uncomfortable against your back in a pack basket.

Select a basket about eighteen inches high. Models higher than this raise the center of gravity of the canoe too much. Place the basket inside an old, waterproof army clothes bag and put this combination into a number 2 Duluth pack. Here you have another waterproof unit, and one that will not gouge your back.

Unfortunately, an outfit like this is expensive, running around fifty dollars for basket, pack, and waterproof liner. Here's a less expensive solution: the next time you go discount-store shopping, take your Duluth pack with you (so what if you look a little crazy; most canoeists are, anyhow). Now, when you pass the housewares section, try to find

FIGURE 36. *The Adirondack Pack Basket*. Items which are breakable or which might be uncomfortable in a conventional pack sack are placed in the pack basket. To make a watertight unit, the basket is first placed in a waterproof army clothes bag.

a plastic trash can that fits inside your Duluth pack. A trash can of somewhat squarish dimensions usually fits comfortably. The cheaper the trash can, the better. The cheaper cans tend to be more flimsy, and hence conform better to your bony contours than more expensive, rigid models. When you find a plastic can that fits—buy it!

You can line the cover of the trash can with rubber auto stripping to make a watertight seal, but it is just as easy to insert the can into a waterproof bag. It is best to insert the trash can in the bag, not vice versa. This way sharp objects within the pack won't puncture the waterproof liner. Finally, insert the whole combo in a number 2 Duluth pack.

WATERPROOF PACK LINERS

You would think the age of synthetics, technology, and gadgetry could produce a decently sized, rugged, waterproof bag. To date, the most suitable liner for a Duluth pack that is tough enough for extended tripping is the old waterproof army clothes bag. Even the army bag is too small to be a good fit in a number 3 Duluth pack and will have to be modified to accept a larger load. Buy your waterproof bags from a local surplus store on a day when you have a lot of time on your hands—you will spend that time searching for a few bags in reasonably good condition. Most bags will have tiny pinholes in them; you can find these by putting the bag over your head in a strong light. Any bag with less than ten holes is a good deal. Use silver duct tape or inner-tube patches to seal the holes. When you get home, lengthen the bag by sewing a strip of waterproof nylon around the top. Add several ties. Turn the modified bag inside out and tape all seams with duct tape. When it's in use the bag is filled with clothing or equipment, and the nylon strip on top is rolled down to form a tight seal. The ties are tied together over the rolled-down top. A little experimenting will show you how to roll the top for maximum efficiency. This is the most versatile, durable, and watertight system I've found, and it is also quite inexpensive.

COMMERCIAL WATERPROOF BAGS

Camp-Paks, by Voyageur Enterprises, are perhaps the most efficient, reliable, and reasonably priced waterproof gear bags currently available. A Camp-Pak consists of an 11-mil-thick, waterproof, polyethylene inner

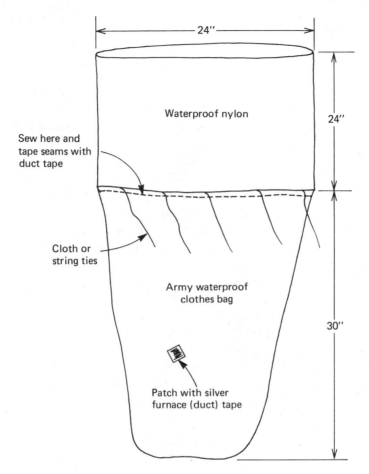

FIGURE 37. *Modifying a Waterproof Army Clothes Bag*

bag, and a woven, tear- and puncture-proof, polypropylene outer bag. The unit, which is sealed with a sliding Versa-Seal closure, is absolutely waterproof. Voyageur bags come in two sizes: 22 by 36 (the V2 model), and 24-by-60 (the V16 model). If you canoe rough rivers you will like these bags, as they provide very dependable protection for your equipment. Unfortunately, Voyageur bags are extremely awkward to carry, since their odd sizes prevent their being used inside Duluth packs. A reasonably efficient method of carrying these bags is to lash them to a pack frame. Such an arrangement is considerably less handy than Duluth packs with interior waterproof liners, but provides a good, inexpensive solution to the problem faced by the canoeist who also backpacks.

WATERPROOF CAMERA BAGS

Canoeists are great storytellers. It's too bad most of them (myself included) don't have pictures to back up their whopping good tales. Usually canoeists dismiss photo requests with a simple comment like, "No way am I gonna take my four-hundred-dollar camera on a canoe trip and dump it in the river." And there is much wisdom in that statement. Although many paddlers carry expensive cameras on canoe trips, most keep them well hidden in the bottom of watertight packs and bring them out around suppertime when all the gear is unpacked (this explains all the pictures of happy campers sitting around the fire eating).

White-water paddlers commonly stow their cameras in 50-caliber ammunition boxes (army surplus). This is a fine solution, but ammo boxes are heavy and cumbersome on portages, and the loud snapping noise of the lid-latch frightens away wildlife.

An almost ideal camera bag can be found on the shelves of your army surplus store. It's called a gas-mask bag. It's just the right size, absolutely watertight, light, and extremely rugged. Moreover, it opens and closes easily. You can strap the bag to your hip on portages and have your camera with you at all times. A few commercial manufacturers make less sturdy copies of gas-mask bags, and they are expensive. For the past ten years gas-mask bags have been selling for around three dollars.

TENTS

Traditionally, canoeists have always carried much heavier loads than backpackers. This is because you can put a lot more weight in a canoe than on your back. Carrying sixty-five pounds over a half-mile portage is not much more strenuous than carrying fifty. Obviously, the difference widens as the distance increases. But the canoeist is not usually faced with many long portages. Long carries like the Grand Portage in Minnesota (nine miles) and the Methye Portage in Canada (thirteen miles) are the exception rather than the rule. Most paddlers will never carry a canoe and equipment more than a mile.

Consequently, canoeists can afford to carry a bit more weight than backpackers, and some of this additional weight can be in the tent. If you have a lightweight tent for backpacking, you may want to use it on your canoe trips, but the greater comfort of a larger, heavier tent will more than make up for the effort of carrying it. I'm not advocating a forty-pound canvas cottage, but a seven-by-nine nylon tent which weighs between ten and fifteen pounds. Numerous tents like this are available.

In choosing a model take into account that in canoe-camping tents are usually pitched on sand or gravel bars, mud flats, or solid rock. It is very difficult (and frustrating) to set up conventionally designed "U-stake 'em" tents on such terrain. Only occasionally will you be lucky enough to find a tent site with real grass. Well-designed frame tents like the Eureka Drawtite and Timberline, Bishop Ultimate, and Jan Sport Dome set up quickly and easily on any type of ground and are very wind-stable. This is an important consideration because camps are often

FIGURE 38. *The Best Canoe Tents Are Those with Self-Supporting Frames.* This 7' x 9' Eureka Drawtite tent is shown pitched on solid rock (no stakes necessary). The tent weighs about 15 pounds with nylon construction, and about 23 pounds with cotton-canvas construction. (*Photo courtesy of Eureka Tent Co.*)

pitched in the open where welcome winds blow away bothersome mosquitoes and black flies.

Just because a tent is self-supporting doesn't mean you don't have to stake it. A high wind can turn an improperly anchored tent into a kite. Good self-supporting tents can be securely anchored with only four to six stakes—about half the number required to secure conventional style tents. For this reason they are almost universally preferred by experienced canoe trippers.

The only suitable tent material is nylon. Cotton tents are too heavy; they gain weight when wet, and they mildew. When you buy a nylon tent, make sure you specify two-ply construction. This means that the tent consists of two layers of fabric. The main tent body is built of a porous nylon or mosquito net, to let body-produced water vapor out. To keep the rain from getting in, a chemically coated waterproof *fly* is suspended a few inches over the inner tent. The result is a shelter that is completely watertight, breathable, and lightweight. You can pitch the tent without the fly on clear nights, or you can remove the rain-fly and use it separately as your only shelter for camping in the fall when bugs are no problem.

THE TARPAULIN (RAIN-FLY)

No canoeist should be without a nylon tarp (sometimes called a rain-fly). The rain-fly is not for waterproofing tents; it is for waterproofing people. When the rains come erect your tarp, place your equipment under it, and fire up the stove. For greatest versatility, select a rain-fly about ten feet square, or larger if you prefer. Look for polymer- or urethane-coated nylon fabric in 2- to 3-ounce weight per square yard. Although you can find tarps built of 1.5-ounce nylon and lighter, the heavier weight is best as it possesses much more reserve strength. When you get your fly, customize it as shown in figure 39. You will then be able to use it more efficiently under a greater variety of conditions.

Pitching the Rain-Fly

You can pitch a rain-fly in an unlimited number of geometric configurations. There are so many possible patterns that most people don't know how to rig a single wind-stable design quickly. When you see storm

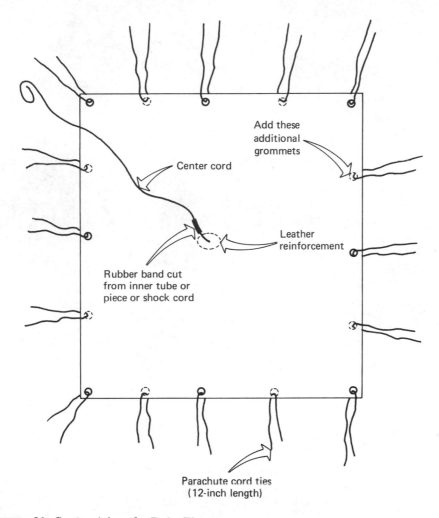

Add these
additional
grommets

Center cord

Leather
reinforcement

Rubber band cut
from inner tube or
piece or shock cord

Parachute cord ties
(12-inch length)

FIGURE 39. *Customizing the Rain-Fly*

clouds moving in, feel the temperature drop, and suddenly everything becomes still, you generally have only a few minutes to get some rain-cover
over your gear. The majority of campers are pretty haphazard about
fly pitching, and as a result the first good wind that comes along rips the
corner grommets right out of the fly. Consequently, some canoeists believe that tarps should never be set up in a wind-driven rain. Unfortunately, this is when you need their protection most.

After years of experimenting, I've come to prefer this simple, strong,
and efficient method of rigging (figures 40a and 40b).

FIGURE 40a and FIGURE 40b. *A Simple and Sturdy Method of Pitching a Rain-Fly*

MATERIALS
A fly customized like the one shown in figure 39
50 feet of nylon rope
6 lightweight aluminum tent stakes
2 trees, not over 30 feet apart

PROCEDURE
1. Locate 2 trees about 15–20 feet apart. String a drum-tight line between the trees about 5 feet off the ground. Use 2 half-hitches at one end of the rope and a power-cinch with a quick release knot at the other end (see Chapter 9 for a review of knots). Leave about 10 feet of free rope at each knot.

2. Take the pair of ties at one corner of your fly and wind one tie of the set around the rope in a clockwise direction and the other tie in a counterclockwise direction. Take at least 4 turns around the rope. Secure the ties with a simple overhand bow.

3. Pull the other corner of the open end of the fly tight along the rope and secure it with the ties, as in number 2 above. The tie wrappings will provide sufficient tension to keep the corners of the tarp from slipping inward along the rope when the fly is buffeted by wind.

4. Secure all remaining ties to the rope with a simple overhand bow. (By securing the fly at several points along the length of its open end, rather than just at the corners, as is commonly done, you distribute the strain across a wide area, thus increasing the strength of the fly.)

5. Go to the back of the fly, pull it out tight, and stake.

6. Run the center cord over a tree limb or a rope strung just above and behind the fly. Snug up the center cord (use a power-cinch with a quick-release knot) to pull the center of the fly out.

7. Take the 10 feet or so of free rope at each tree and run it through the center side grommets of the tarp. Pull the ropes through each grommet as far as possible and tie a simple half-hitch at the grommet. Stake the free ends of these ropes to the ground. This will put the sides of the fly under some tension. You now have a very sturdy, rain-free shelter that won't flap in the wind.

GROUND CLOTH

Now that tents come with sewn-in floors, many canoeists omit plastic ground cloths from their equipment. Frankly, I think this is a mistake. I always line the *inside* of my tent with a ground cloth made from Visqueen plastic (available at low cost from any lumber yard). I make my ground cloth just a few inches larger than the tent floor so that it will "flow" up the sides of the tent a bit. If my tent springs a leak during a heavy rain, the water will run under the plastic sheet and I will remain perfectly dry. Without the ground sheet you have no control over water which enters your tent while you are asleep.

If you put your ground cloth between the tent floor and the ground, rain striking the tent will fall to the plastic and slither under the tent where it will become trapped. Ultimately, this trapped water will wick its way up through the bottom of the tent. You will really have a sponge party if this happens.

SLEEPING GEAR

A sleeping bag is an item of clothing, not equipment. You *wear* a sleeping bag—you don't *use* it. If you want to be warm and comfortable in the outdoors you must choose your wearing apparel wisely, and sleeping bags are no exception.

DOWN-FILLED SLEEPING BAGS

A good-quality sleeping bag, filled with sufficient duck or goose down to keep you comfortably warm in temperatures well below freezing, will weigh around four pounds and stuff into a waterproof carrying sack scarcely larger than a two-pound coffee can. These characteristics— warmth, light weight, and compactness—have made down-insulated sleeping bags a popular choice among wilderness canoeists.

However, down-filled bags are expensive, drying wet down is difficult, and down has a tendency to absorb moisture in humid weather. As down bags absorb water, their loft (thickness) decreases and their weight increases. On a humid or hot, sweaty night, a down bag can absorb several ounces of water from the air or your body. Ultimately, the interior atmosphere of the bag will become muggy. Camping along river bottoms is, by nature, a muggy experience, and down bags compound the problem. For this reason, I am coming to prefer the efficient new synthetics.

SYNTHETIC-FILLED SLEEPING BAGS

Avid wilderness campers are in agreement that the only suitable substitutes for down are Dupont's Polyester Fiberfill II and Celanese's Polarguard. From the standpoint of thermal efficiency, it takes about 1.4 pounds of Fiberfill or Polarguard to equal a pound of down. Average canoe-country temperatures seldom go below thirty-two degrees Fahrenheit, and in this climate a bag filled with 1½ pounds of good down or 2 pounds of Fiberfill II or Polarguard is very adequate. In fact, I would rule out as *too warm* any closely fitting bag with much more filler than this.

A bag filled with 2 pounds of Fiberfill II or Polarguard will weigh between 3½ and 4½ pounds, and will stuff into a sack of 9-by-18 inches, which is very suitable for canoeing. Additionally, the cost of such a bag will be considerably less than a comparable down-filled model.

Another important advantage of Fiberfill and Polarguard is that these synthetic materials, unlike down, stubbornly refuse to absorb water. If a Fiberfill or Polarguard bag gets wet it can be wrung out and, like wool, will retain a good share of its warmth. Down, on the other hand, possesses almost no insulating value when water-soaked.

In spite of the advantages of these new materials, you may like down-filled sleeping bags because of their excellent draping qualities (if you've ever slept under a feather-and-down comforter you know what I mean). Buy what you can afford; but whatever you buy, make sure it has a hood to keep your head warm (this is where most of your body-heat is lost), and a full-length two-way zipper to keep your feet cool. In addition, the smaller the bag, the lighter it will be, and the less area you will have to heat to keep warm. For these reasons you should select a fairly close-fitting bag with a tapered mummy shape.

Obviously, if you commonly share your bag with someone, a pair of zip-together semirectangular sleepers will be the best choice. The inefficiency of these larger, harder-to-heat bags will be more than compensated for by the warmth of togetherness.

CUSTOMIZING A BADLY DESIGNED SLEEPING BAG

What do you do if you have an old, heavy, not very efficient rectangular sleeping bag and you can't afford to buy a new one? You customize it, that's what.

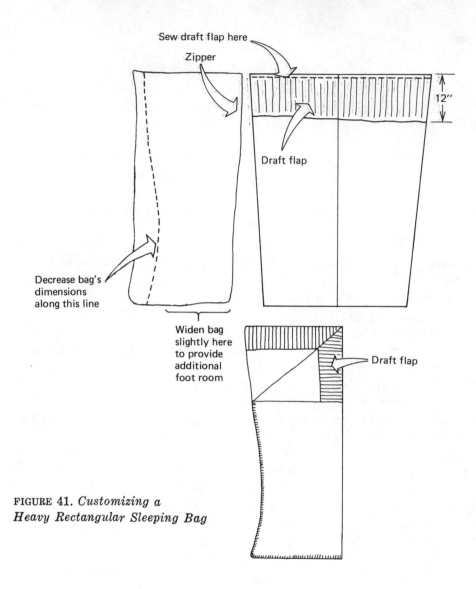

FIGURE 41. *Customizing a Heavy Rectangular Sleeping Bag*

To make a bulky, overweight bag warmer and lighter, decrease its dimensions along the lines shown in figure 41. The easiest way to determine the proper dimensions for you is to climb into the bag and snuggle up right against the zipper. Have a friend push in the material on the side opposite the zipper until it barely touches your body. Then push the material back out about 4 inches and mark with chalk, tape, or pins. Climb out of the bag and sew along the marked line. Cut off the excess fabric, bind the raw edges with seam tape, and your *new* sleeping bag is complete. If the sewing sounds like too much work, take the bag to a tent-and-awning maker or shoe repair man. These professionals can complete a simple sewing job like this in a few minutes on their heavy-duty machines, and the cost will be nominal.

Next, install a 12-inch-wide draft flap around the neck area of the bag to keep warmth in and cold out. Make the draft flap out of cotton flannel and sew it directly to the top of the bag as shown in figure 41.

These simple alterations will reduce the weight of an average nine-pound "station wagon" bag by about three pounds, and will extend its temperature range by at least ten degrees.

A good way to make a very light, acceptably warm bag for average canoe-trip conditions is to buy a Thermaliner sleeping bag liner (available from L. L. Bean, Inc.). The Thermaliner is similar to the Sportsman's Space Blanket, except that the material breathes. Made from Dupont's Tyvek Olefin fabric, it is soft and flexible. The product has been on the market for several years but for some reason has not attained much popularity. Nevertheless, it makes a very versatile, compact sleeping bag if teamed with a lightweight, loosely woven blanket. If you are sleeping on a foam pad inside a tent, this combination should keep you reasonably warm down to about fifty degrees (tent temperatures generally run about eight to ten degrees warmer than outside temperatures).

MATTRESSES

When temperatures are much below fifty degrees, an air mattress is unsuitable. The air in an air mattress is continually moving from one tube to another, ever so slightly; if the ground is cold, this cold will be transmitted right to your bones. You will, in effect, be sleeping on a re-circulating refrigerator. Down, especially, compresses to almost nothing, and to a lesser extent, so do Fiberfill II and Polarguard. This is less of a problem with old-style kapok- or wool-filled sleeping bags, because the filler in these bags is so thick and uncompressible that an effective insulative layer is created between your back and the air mattress. The price you pay for this thermal barrier is weight and overall rolled size; hence the popularity of smaller and lighter bags.

For adequate warmth in early spring, you must have some kind of insulation between your back and the cold ground. Either open-cell urethane or closed-cell Ensolite foam is satisfactory. I prefer breathable urethane for comfort, and I especially like a cotton cover on my pad. Pads covered with waterproof nylon do not permit the free passage of air and water vapor, and thus get very hot in warm weather. If you use a waterproof pad in temperatures much above fifty degrees, you will wake up in the morning with a drenched back; cotton-covered pads are much cooler and make for a more restful night.

For the ultimate in comfort and insulation in cool weather, team a nylon air mattress with a quarter-inch-thick Ensolite pad. This combo weighs about four pounds but is very compact. The comfort is worth the extra weight.

If you're on a budget, visit your local carpet store and buy a piece of carpet padding about 62 inches long and 20 inches wide. Carpet padding works great as a mattress and is much less expensive than store-bought pads. Additionally, carpet pads are ideal if you are canoeing with toddlers who wet their sleeping gear every night. In the morning you need only rinse the wet pad in clean water and hang it in the sun to dry. Although nylon-covered pads seem attractive for toddlers, in practice they don't work well. The youngsters roll, slide, and squirm right off them. An uncovered pad produces more friction and keeps children moderately immobile.

PILLOW

For me, at least, a pillow is a necessity. I use one of the very light, air-filled, nylon models, which cost only a few dollars. Unless you are very hardheaded, a pillow will save many headaches.

STUFF SACKS

The best way to organize items is to place them in color-coded, waterproof, nylon stuff sacks. Make a variety of different-size stuff sacks and install drawstrings to tie them shut.

Traditionally, I place all my personal clothing for a canoe trip into a lobster-red nylon sack about 8 inches wide by 19 inches long. I make waterproof sacks for the repair kit, cook set, first-aid kit, rain gear, and foodstuffs like Bisquick and pancake mix (food sacks are first lined with plastic Zip-Lock bags).

When placed in a waterproof liner inside a Duluth pack, nylon stuff sacks provide additional waterproofing insurance. They are also convenient for keeping your things dry while packing or unpacking in a rain. In early spring, waterproof stuff sacks are indispensible.

COOKING GEAR

For a party of four you will need the following cooking equipment:

Group Equipment

3½-quart aluminum pot with cover
3-quart aluminum pot with cover
6-cup coffee pot
9½-inch cast aluminum or stainless steel frying pan
oven (see discussion below)
2-quart graduated plastic shaker with cover
waterproof salt and pepper shakers
spatula with 4–6-inch-long handle
aluminum pot lifter (or small pliers)
stainless steel Sierra Club cup for use as a soup ladle, extra cup, or bowl
waterproof stuff sack to store the cook kit

Personal Equipment

insulated or stainless steel cup
plastic cereal bowl
spoon
fork
pocket knife

If you snap your Sierra Cup to a brass hook attached to the outside of your Duluth pack, you won't have to unpack the cook kit when you need a cup for lunch or a drink of water. A good idea is to keep the graduated plastic shaker tied to a canoe thwart, where it will become a handy bailer if your canoe takes too much water in heavy waves or rapids. Use the shaker for mixing Kool-Aid, measuring water for soup, or whipping instant pudding. The inscribed graduations enable you to determine the precise amounts of water needed to reconstitute freeze-dried and dehydrated foods.

OVENS

In the days of large campfires, I used a folding reflector oven for all my baking. Now, however, I cook on a stove or small fire, so the polished aluminum reflector is out of place. I use a Bendonn aluminum dutch oven, which consists of two modified frying pans and a pair of spring steel handles. One pan is inverted over the other and hot coals are placed in a special ring on top. Pastries within the oven cook from the heat above. Additionally, this versatile cooker can be used to pop corn, fry potatoes, and boil soup. It weighs only 25 ounces, and will nest compactly with most cook kits.

You can easily make an acceptable Dutch oven by inverting a large frying pan over a smaller one, or by placing a skillet or cake pan on top of a pot. Put your bake-stuff in the oven and build a small, hot fire on the cover. Use almost no heat on the bottom. Best results will be obtained if you set this homemade unit in the warm ashes. Because Dutch ovens receive heat from above rather than below, burning is seldom a problem. Bisquick bread or blueberry muffins will cook in about thirty minutes if plenty of heat is used.

STOVES

For most kinds of canoe-camping a stove is a necessity. Scrounging for wood on a denuded, overused campsite is not conducive to having a good time, and neither is the inconvenience of cooking in the rain. Fire bans, too, can be a problem. You never know when the forest service will disallow fires for reasons of low humidity and inadequate rainfall. Although the traditional campfire has not yet been abolished in most wilderness areas, it is disappearing. There simply isn't enough wood available to support the number of campers who want to build fires. Then, too, in many locales all land adjacent to rivers is privately owned, and fire building is strictly prohibited.

If you are on a limited budget and must choose between a camp stove and an ax and saw, choose the stove. The cost will be about the same—not to mention the labor you will save by not chopping down the forest.

Gasoline Stoves

When selecting a stove, remember that canoeing is not backpacking. You can afford to carry a bigger, more powerful, and more reliable stove than a backpacker. For the past four years I have been using an

Optimus 111B gasoline stove. This one-burner, pump-equipped "blow torch" weighs 3½ pounds, is extremely rugged, and absolutely reliable under virtually any conditions. The stove is also quite economical to operate. I used the 111B exclusively on a twenty-one-day trip to James Bay in 1974 (I built a fire only twice). I prepared food for six people, made popcorn, and heated dishwater—and used only two gallons of gas on the entire trip.

I am also very fond of the tiny Svea-Optimus (Primus) stoves, which are commonly sold in backpacking shops. These stoves are quite adequate for canoeing and they put out good heat. But they lack a really stable pot support, are temperamental, and not very wind-proof. Nevertheless, any one of these stoves is a good investment and will give you years of good service.

Starting a small Svea or Optimus stove can be a problem because no pump is provided to generate pressure (an optional minipump is available at extra cost). The lighting instructions furnished with this type of stove tell you to cup the tank in your hands, warming it slightly, to provide sufficient pressure for starting. An easier way is to prime the stove with an eye dropper. Just suck some gas out of the tank with the dropper and squirt it below the burner plate. Cap the stove tightly, light the gas, and stand back. When the flame is almost burned out, turn up the heat.

For serious wilderness trips I always carry a small Svea stove in addition to my 111B. Although I don't often use the Svea, it's good to have a second burner—just in case the infallible Optimus 111B proves fallible!

The best way to carry gas is in liter-size (1 liter equals 1.06 quarts) SIGG aluminum bottles. These bottles, which tend to be rather expensive, are available at almost every camping shop. A cheaper solution is to use the heavy plastic Gerry Jugs designed especially for gasoline. These gallon jugs are absolutely leak-proof, almost indestructible, and cost only a few dollars. I have used two such containers on three one-week trips with teenagers and they are still in fine shape. Any product which hangs together after three weeks in the hands of fourteen-year-olds is to be highly recommended.

I generally allow two liters of gas per week for a party of four to six people (not including the original stove-tank filling). This is plenty of gas if you don't waste it by running your stove indiscriminately.

Butane Stoves

In recent years a number of simple-to-operate butane gas stoves have appeared on the market. These stoves require no pumping, no priming, and no pouring of gas. Just turn the adjuster knob and light. Unfortunately, butane stoves don't put out much heat, and most work poorly unless they are well shielded from the wind. The heating efficiency of bottled butane is directly related to the outside temperature—the warmer the temperature, the greater the gas pressure, and the better the stove performs. If the temperature drops much below freezing, the butane will liquify and the stove won't start. Then there is the problem of what to do with the spent gas containers. Obviously you can't leave them lying all over the woods, and you can't bury them, so the only solution is to pack them out. On a long trip you may have to carry up to a dozen fuel cylinders, which is certainly less convenient than a single gallon can of gasoline.

You won't find experienced wilderness canoeists using butane stoves. They're okay for two- or 3-day local trips, but stick with gasoline or kerosine for serious ventures.

Kerosine Stoves

Kerosine stoves are very efficient and economical to operate. They are also safe to use, mainly because kerosine is less volatile than gas. Unfortunately, kerosine stoves cannot be started unless they are first primed with alcohol or gasoline, and they don't burn as hot as comparable gas models.

Sterno and Alcohol Stoves

These are good for keeping food warm. Avoid them for serious cooking—three or four candles work about as well.

A final thought regarding stoves. Keep one-burner models in a light cotton or nylon stuff sack when not in use. This will keep lint and dust out of the burner parts and will protect the stove from dents and scratches. If your stove has a pump, be sure to include some oil in your repair kit to lubricate the leather pump washer.

CUTLERY

Knives

I have a great aversion to sheath knives on canoe trips. Granted, they look woodsy, but they are uncomfortable to wear in a canoe; the knife handle gets caught in your life jacket and the tip of the sheath catches on the seat, and so on. If you upset in rapids and your leather sheath gets wet, you will feel like you are carrying a slab of bacon on your hip. Besides, sheathing a knife in wet leather is just asking for rust problems.

Many seasoned canoeists prefer a heavy-duty pocket knife with one or two blades about 3 to 4 inches long. Choose a knife with thin, finely pointed blades, and specify stainless steel—a must for use around water. Stick to good-quality American-made knives like Case, Gerber, Shrade Walden, Western, Buck, and Camillus. In spite of what you may have heard about legendary foreign steels, we Americans make the best mass-produced knives in the world—at any price. My favorite knife, a Gerber, has one 3½-inch-long blade. I carry it in a special snap pocket sewn into my field pants.

If you plan to catch fish, include a fillet knife with your equipment. Don't wear the knife on your hip; rather, store it in your pack basket for the ultimate in safety.

Ax and Saw

Axes are still necessary on canoe trips, even though the tree-felling, cabin-building days are over. You need an ax for splitting kindling, driving stubborn tent stakes, setting rivets in torn pack straps, and repairing bent aluminum canoes. But you *don't* need a big ax. Many of our nation's most able woodsmen—Daniel Boone, Davy Crockett, and Jim Bridger—depended entirely on a not-very-efficient tomahawk for all their camping chores. If you saw your wood into 10-inch lengths, you will have no trouble splitting them with a good hand ax.

Perhaps more useful than a hand ax in the lowlands of the far north is a Swedish Brush Ax (Woodsman's Pal). This interesting tool com-bines the power of a hatchet with the blade of a machete. There is even a brush hook at one end. Where a good deal of overgrown vegetation must be cleared along portage trails, this or a machete will be useful.

Whatever edged tool you select, keep it well sheathed when not in use. Most sheaths that come with cutlery are much too thin. To make a knife or ax sheath, obtain some heavy sole leather and soak it in water for ten minutes or until it is flexible. While the leather is wet, mold and cut it to the shape of the tool (you should make a paper pattern first). When the leather is moderately dry, glue the sheath together with contact cement. Seal the protective edges of the sheath with hammer or pop rivets; or, if you prefer, your shoemaker can sew the sheath for you for a dollar or two.

Whetstone

You can't put a good edge on a knife with the stones commonly sold in hardware stores. For an adequate job only an Arkansas stone will do, and these are obtainable at better sporting goods stores everywhere. They are not expensive. I like my knives razor-sharp, so I carry both a coarse (soft) and fine (hard) Arkansas stone and a bottle of special honing oil. You don't need all this, but a fast-cutting soft Arkansas stone is a necessity.

Incidentally, the small butcher's steels commonly available are fine for touching up a knife's edge. They cannot, however, be used for sharpening, as they don't really remove steel; they just realign the microscopic teeth on a knife's edge. Only a stone possesses the abrasive properties necessary to remove metal, and for this reason should not be omitted in favor of a steel.

FOOTWEAR

Canoeists are not in complete agreement as to the most suitable footwear for canoe trips. There is, however, universal agreement among seasoned trippers that leather boots should be avoided. For casual outings and most white-water canoeing, canvas sneakers are almost universally used. These inexpensive shoes provide good protection, are very light and easy to swim in, and dry quickly. But for serious tripping you should choose from the following:

1. Rubber boots with steel shanks and ten- to twelve-inch-high tops—preferred mostly by arctic travelers, who often wade icy rivers.

2. Rubber-bottom–leather-top shoe-pacs of the L.L. Bean type—popular with canoeists who want more support and comfort than that provided by all-rubber boots.

3. Vietnam (Jungle) boots—liked by guides in the rocky Quetico-Superior country of Minnesota and Canada. These canvas-top–leather-bottom boots have heavy-lugged soles, steel shanks, and breathable mesh liners. Since jungle boots were designed for stomping through rice paddies in Vietnam, they are well adapted to the wet, swampy conditions often encountered on a canoe trip. Once they are wet, Vietnam boots dry quickly—generally within an hour, in warm weather. Because their ten-inch-high tops offer good protection from leeches and other pests, these boots are a good choice for Georgia and Florida swamp trips. Vietnam boots are very inexpensive and extremely rugged. Virtually every military surplus store carries a good supply of them.

After years of experimenting, I am won over completely to the L. L. Bean shoe-pac. These boots can be had with tops up to sixteen inches high (I prefer six-inch tops) and with light, medium, or heavyweight bottoms. I have found that pacs with medium-weight bottoms are very adequate, even though they look and feel as if they won't take much abuse. I carry 2 pairs of leather insoles for my pacs. If one pair of insoles gets wet, I merely remove them from the rubber boot bottoms and install a dry pair.

For wilderness canoeing you need an extra pair of boots or shoes. A pair of sneakers for wading or in-camp use is fine, and so is a pair of comfortable leather moccasins. I prefer two pairs of shoe-pacs; a mediumweight pair for general use, and a very supple, lightweight pair for relaxing.

PERSONAL CLOTHING

For one- or 2-day trips, bring a complete change of clothes. For outings longer than two days, add two changes of underwear and three or four pairs of socks. Be sure to take a mediumweight wool jac-shirt or knitted wool sweater and a cotton or nylon windbreaker. There is no need to take additional clothing. Canoe-country temperatures seldom go much below freezing and you can always put on your extra clothes if you get cold.

Regardless of the clothing you select, it should be unrestrictive to allow freedom for paddling. Shirts and jackets should be comfortable to wear under a life jacket. For this reason, bulky down and fiberfill jackets are not recommended. Jacket hoods too, can be a nuisance; in a wind they may blow about your face and obscure your vision. Your canoeing wardrobe should consist almost exclusively of wool for warmth and quick-drying nylon for wind and water protection. Cotton is acceptable only for parkas or for use in very warm weather. You can find good buys on wool garments, cotton ski parkas, army field jackets (the forerunner of modern mountain parkas), fatigues, and field pants at military surplus stores.

WOOLEN LONG JOHNS

Woolen long johns are unnecessary for canoe trips in most of the lower states, but are essential for trips into Canada or Alaska or for any April, May, or early June trips in the far northern states. Many wilderness trippers prefer wide-mesh cotton net underwear to traditional wool longies because the netting provides better ventilation and greater comfort under wider temperature conditions. Unfortunately, net undergarments won't keep you warm when wet, and if you spill in the icy water of a northern waterway, your comfort—and possibly your survival—may well depend upon the insulative value of your clothing.

A seldom-mentioned virtue of scratchy woolen long johns is their ability to almost completely eliminate black fly bites (nothing *completely* eliminates them). These pesky insects, so common in the far north, have an uncanny ability to find the smallest patch of unprotected skin. The solution is to cover up completely, and good, heavy long johns help considerably. Many old-time woodsmen carry rubber bands and secure their pants legs at the ankles to prevent the tiny flies from crawling up their legs and biting. Rubber-banded trousers do reduce black fly bites, but they are less effective than closely woven, tight-fitting long johns.

For cold-water safety and to minimize fly bites (longies won't eliminate mosquito bites, but repellents will), get the heaviest underwear you can find. Inexpensive army surplus woolens are ideal, if you can stand them next to your skin (a good wash with Woolite and fabric softener will reduce the abrasiveness somewhat).

RAIN GEAR

The best rain gear is a two-piece coated nylon rain suit. Ponchos and below-the-knee rain shirts are easy to put on and take off, and are well ventilated, but they are dangerous in a canoe, for in the event of an upset, they make swimming difficult. While a rain suit is more bother than over-the-head rain clothes, it is much safer. The biggest objection to rain suits is the lack of ventilation of the waterproof pants. If you engage in strenuous activity while wearing rain pants, your legs will become soaking wet from the water which condenses on the inside of the coated nylon. This can be a problem if you are backpacking. When canoeing, though, you sit or kneel and hardly use your legs at all, so overheating and condensation is rarely a problem.

Incidentally, some rain trousers are equipped with snaps or velcro at the ankle. Avoid these closures, as they severely restrict ventilation.

EQUIPMENT LIST FOR TWO PERSONS FOR A TRIP OF
ONE WEEK OR MORE

GROUP EQUIPMENT

tent (preferably with self-supporting framework)
plastic ground cloth
10x10-foot (or larger) coated nylon rain-fly
3 Duluth packs (#3 size) or 2 Duluth packs and 1 pack basket
waterproof liners for Duluth packs
100 feet of ¼ inch nylon rope (two 50-foot coils)
100 feet of nylon parachute cord
1 all-steel hand ax
1 compact folding saw
repair and miscellaneous kit:
    1 small pliers with wire cutter, 1 roll fine copper wire, 1 roll silver duct tape, needles, thread, instant epoxy, 12-inch square of fiberglass cloth for canoe or paddle patching, 6 hammer-driven rivets, 2 aluminum carabiners, 1 nylon pulley, small file for sharpening ax, soft Arkansas stone, oil, 3-inch square of scrap canvas for repair, 2-inch square of heavy leather for repair, sharp sewing awl, safety pins, sandpaper
6 heavy-duty rubber ropes with steel hooks attached

large sponge for bailing
thermos for coffee
fillet knife
cook kit and oven
graduated plastic shaker (2 quart)
folding plastic water jug (2½ gallon)
biodegradable soap and abrasive pad for dishwashing
stove and gasoline
matches: carry 3 separate supplies of wooden stick matches, each in a
    screw-cap plastic jar. Place each supply in a different pack.
4 or more candles
folding candle lantern
first-aid kit in waterproof box:
    Band-Aids, butterfly strips, Telfa pads, 2-inch wide roller gauze, ad-
    hesive tape, antiseptic soap swabs, Bacitracin ointment, tweezers,
    scissors, antacid tablets, aspirin, toothache medicine, Chapstick,
    Moleskin for blisters, Compazine (5 mg. tablets) for nausea or
    vomiting, thermometer, water purification tablets, poison ivy cream,
    ammonia inhalent, needle for removing splinters, first-aid manual

INDIVIDUAL EQUIPMENT

life jacket (vest type)
sleeping bag and foam pad
2 pairs of military fatigues or field pants (choose light wool pants in
    spring and fall)
cotton webbed belt (dries faster than leather when wet)
2 lightweight, long-sleeved wool shirts
1 medium-weight wool jac-shirt, or medium-weight knitted wool sweater
1 cotton T-shirt
1 pair woolen long johns (spring, fall, and all arctic trips)
4 pairs medium-weight wool socks (at least 75% wool content)
1 cotton or nylon wind parka (not waterproof)
1 waterproof 2-piece rain suit
1 brimmed felt hat (for arctic trips add a wool stocking cap)
extra glasses if you wear them
sunglasses
security strap for glasses
3 pairs nylon undershorts (nylon dries faster than cotton and is warmer)

1 towel (old baby diaper is ideal)
2 red bandannas
1 pair rubber-bottom boots
1 pair sneakers, moccasins, or other soft footwear for camp use
1 pair lightweight leather gloves (for arctic trips use leather-faced wool
    or plastic-coated cotton gloves)
1 flashlight, extra bulb and batteries
heavy-duty pocket knife
toiletries (include hand lotion for chapped hands)
compass (orienteering style)
map set in waterproof case
butane lighter (handy for relighting stoves, candles, etc; saves matches)
insect repellent—at least 2 bottles. (Hint: repackaging repellent in
    empty roll-on deodorant containers enables you to apply just the
    right amount of repellent in just the right places, with only one
    hand.)
wristwatch
2 insect head nets—for protection against mosquitoes and black flies.
    Head nets are a must for arctic and far northern trips and are
    readily available from most military surplus stores. Loss of a head
    net can lead to insanity; always carry two!

OPTIONAL AND INTERESTING ITEMS

Metal Match for emergency fire starting
Fire Ribbon—a chemical for emergency fire starting (at most camp
    shops)
2 red smoke bombs for emergency signaling
air splints for broken limbs (for isolated trips)
1 ultralight mountaineering hammock (rolls to fist size, weighs about 3
    ounces—for general relaxing and can be used to make a stretcher)
1 small pocket thermometer (to settle temperature arguments)
camera and film
fishing gear

PACKING OUT

For a trip of more than a week you will need two #3 Duluth packs
and a 3-peck (18-inch high) pack basket *per canoe*. If you prefer, you

can eliminate the basket and substitute an additional Duluth pack. Canoe partners should pack together as follows:

Duluth Pack #1

Place the two sleeping bags in the bottom of the watertight pack liner. Set your foam pads or air mattresses above this and complete the package with one or two clothes bags (each canoeist should have his or her own clothes bag. This is a 9-x-18-inch waterproof stuff sack into which all your clothes and personal gear is placed).

Seal the waterproof liner of the Duluth pack and put your nylon rain tarp *on top* of the sealed liner. Should a rain come, the tarp will be quickly and easily accessible. Also, by setting the tarp on top, you reduce the chance of leakage at the opening of the waterproof bag if you overturn, because the fly makes a watertight seal when the pack flap is drawn tightly down over it.

Finish by sliding your folding saw, ax, and extra rope down the side of the pack between the waterproof liner and the pack canvas. This will permit quick access to these items without the necessity of breaking the seal of the waterproof liner.   TOTAL PACK WEIGHT—about 35 pounds

Duluth Pack #2

Place the nylon bags containing your food in this pack. Organize soft items so they won't gouge your back. If you select dehydrated and freeze-dried foods, a two-week supply for two people will take up about half the pack. The remaining space can be filled with sundries. Seal the waterproof liner, place your rain gear on top, and cinch down the closing flap.   TOTAL PACK WEIGHT—about 65 pounds

Pack Basket

Place your cook kit, in its protective stuff sack, in the bottom of the pack basket. Atop this set your stove and gasoline, thermos, repair and first-aid kits, fishing reel and lures, and other items which are breakable or might be uncomfortable in a conventional pack. Seal the waterproof liner, set your tent on top of the basket, and cinch down the pack flap.
                    TOTAL PACK WEIGHT—about 45 pounds

PACKING THE CANOE

Place the food pack directly behind the yoke, centered in the canoe. This is your heaviest load and you want it perfectly balanced. Set your pack basket on the other side of the yoke and put your light clothes pack next to the pack on the side of the lightest paddler. This should provide sufficient weight to level the canoe. If a fourth pack is carried, as on extended trips, packs can be placed sideways (parallel to the gunwales) in the canoe. The important thing is to have a low, well-balanced load, with the major portion of the weight as close to the middle of the canoe as possible.

If your tent is very large, you may wish to slide it from under the pack basket flap and set it beneath (and parallel to) the center thwart. Finish loading by installing your shock-corded security system. If you overturn your gear will be locked tightly in place, and if your tent is placed under the center thwart, it will be imprisoned by the packs on either side.

You can pay a great deal of money for sophisticated waterproof bags and fancy packs of all types. However, for reliability and versatility I heartily recommend this packing system. In preparing this section I contacted many super trippers who take 6-week or longer canoe safaris into the arctic. Every individual I spoke with uses this method, or some modification thereof.

A final thought regarding equipment, packing, and loading. If backpackers are a little sloppy in packing, their backs may suffer. But if canoeists are sloppy and get their equipment wet, or, worse, lose it in an upset on an isolated wilderness river, they may be lucky to escape with their lives.

OVER THE PORTAGE AND THROUGH THE WOODS

The standard procedure for portaging is as follows: each person takes a pack and a paddle (the paddle is used as a walking stick) and strikes out across the portage. While walking, both canoeists look for shortcuts back to the river or lake ahead as well as for obstacles that will have to be circuited when the canoe is brought over the trail. Packs are dropped at the end of the portage, and the pair returns. On the second trip one person carries the canoe and the other person takes the last pack and any remaining items. Usually the person with the pack

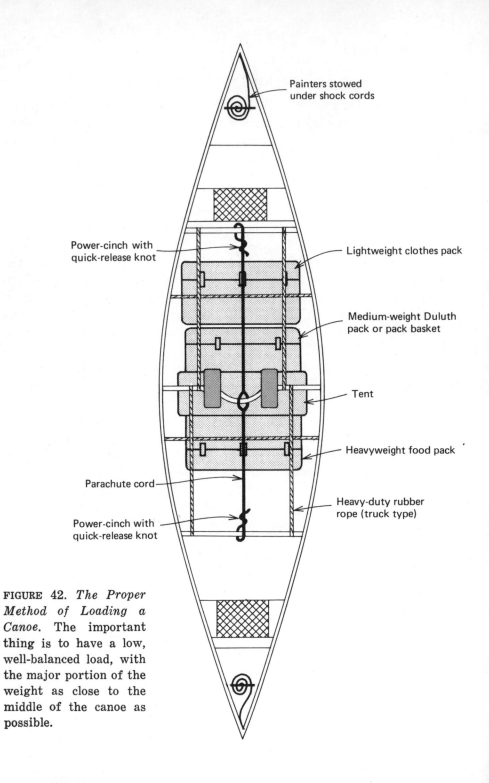

Painters stowed
under shock cords

Power-cinch with
quick-release knot

Lightweight clothes pack

Medium-weight Duluth
pack or pack basket

Tent

Heavyweight food pack

Parachute cord

Power-cinch with
quick-release knot

Heavy-duty rubber
rope (truck type)

FIGURE 42. *The Proper Method of Loading a Canoe.* The important thing is to have a low, well-balanced load, with the major portion of the weight as close to the middle of the canoe as possible.

leads, so that when the canoe-carrier becomes tired he or she can call to the person ahead to look for a suitable stopping place—like an out-jutting tree limb where the bow of the canoe can be set. When such a limb is found, the canoe-carrier sets the bow in place and steps from beneath the yoke to rest. This procedure requires much less energy than setting a canoe on the ground and later lifting it to the shoulders.

In heavily traveled wilderness areas wooden rests are often pro-vided to prevent people from jamming canoe ends into tree branches. Although such rests spoil the primitive nature of the portage, they are essential to minimize environmental damage to foliage. In parklike areas where portages are known to be clear and in good condition, the canoe is sometimes carried over the trail first—primarily because it is the heaviest load and requires the greatest expenditure of energy.

11.
Wilderness
Navigation

Unlike the backpacker, who usually has a marked trail to follow, the canoeist must often travel in a maze of interconnecting lakes and streams. Virtually all of the canoe-country of northern Minnesota, Canada, and New England is comprised of complex, unmarked waterways. In the heavily traveled Boundary Waters Canoe Area of Minnesota (the largest wilderness area east of the Rocky Mountains), signs have been erected at nearly every portage to guide paddlers in their travels. Signs are evident on southern waterways too. Several well-marked canoe trails now wind their way through a jungle of lush greenery in the Florida Everglades—our second largest national park.

Part of the fun of a wilderness canoe trip is the feeling of self-sufficiency, and this feeling disappears when you see your first sign. Nevertheless, the U.S. Forest Service feels that with thousands of inexperienced canoeists now penetrating wilderness areas, markers of some sort are necessary on popular canoe routes to prevent government officials from spending a major portion of their time locating lost persons.

In spite of the presence of directional signs in some wilderness areas, you must still find your own way. On a large lake with many bays, islands, and peninsulas, locating the correct portage, channel, or inlet when there may be half a dozen or more on the same lake, presents enough of a challenge to most canoeists to keep things interesting. There are, of course, many areas where man's influence has not yet penetrated. You will find no signs in northern Canada or Alaska, and if your heart throbs at the thought of an arctic canoe trip, your knowledge of navigation will have to be strictly first-rate. "But I'm not a lake canoeist—I only paddle rivers," you might say. All well and good. You still must be able to read and interpret a river map, and because of variability in water conditions, channel erosion, and the influence of man, interpretation of river guides and maps calls for a much higher degree of resourcefulness than you might imagine. Whether you canoe local rivers or wilderness waterways, you will feel more confident and secure if you understand the basic principles of direction finding.

EQUIPMENT

MAPS

Of foremost importance is the map. Except for going in a straight line, a compass is totally worthless without a map. Get the best topographic maps available; these can be purchased from a variety of sources (see Appendix A—Map Sources). Cost, including postage, seldom runs over $1.25 a sheet. For advance trip planning it is best to write to the U.S. Geological Survey's map distribution office in your area (regional addresses are given in Appendix A). Request a free "Index to Topographic Maps." This index will tell you what maps are currently in print, in what scale, and the cost. If much of your travel will be on large, complex lakes, request the largest scale available. 1:24,000 scale maps are best for picking your way across mazelike lakes, although at this large scale you will need several of them. Smaller 1:50,000 scale maps are ideal for most wilderness canoe travel (the larger the denominator of the scale, the smaller the actual map scale). Usually, however, you can't afford to be so choosy. Large-scale maps are readily available for heavily traveled or civilized areas, while more remote sections of the continent may be available only in small scale. Avoid maps with scales smaller than 1 inch = 2 miles. Such small-scale maps are useful to experts, but they don't inspire confidence in beginners.

Maps drawn especially for canoeists are often available in canoeing guidebooks or may be purchased for a nominal fee from many states' departments of natural resources. Canoeing has grown tremendously popular over the past few years; better maps are sure to follow.

When you have secured your maps, cut and tape (using transparent Scotch tape) the sections together so as to completely cover the area you wish to canoe. Although a large, single map is somewhat cumbersome, it is certainly less bother than several independent map sheets—especially when you find yourself working on the edges of two adjacent sheets. Cover nonwaterproof maps with clear contact paper. The adhesive-backed plastic should be placed over *both* sides of the map sheet to insure a watertight seal. A waterproof map is a *must* for canoeing! If you like more stiffness to your map, purchase some Chartex dry-mounting cloth for the backing from a supplier of engineering and forestry equipment. From the same supplier you can also get a special clear plastic with a slow-curing adhesive designed especially for use with maps. I think you will like the clear contact best, however; although more difficult to work with, it is readily available and less expensive than the special map coverings.

MAP CASE

A map case is a must for nonwaterproof maps and is desirable for waterproof ones as well. There are several good, watertight plastic cases available for under five dollars, and these are certainly worth the money. If your canoe was properly outfitted with shock cords as explained in Chapter 3, your map case can be secured by sliding it under a shock-corded thwart. If rapids will be encountered the free case ends can be snapped or taped together to provide absolute security against loss, or a short piece of nylon cord can be attached to both case and canoe. As previously pointed out, anything which dangles free in a fast-water upset is likely to be sheared off on the nearest rock or log, and loss of maps in the wilderness is cause for serious concern.

THE COMPASS

Buy a decent compass. In fact, buy two, since one can be lost or broken. You don't have to spend a lot of money for a serviceable instru-

FIGURE 43. *Compasses for the Canoeist.* Key: OR = orienteering style compass; FD = floating dial compass; SD = stationary or fixed dial compass; CR = cruiser compass.

Left to Right (top row). (1) Michaels Mapper—OR with declination adjustment. (2) Warren-Knight Cruiser—CR with declination adjustment. (3) Suunto KB-14—optical lensatic FD. (4) Taylor #2912—SD. (5) Pic (made by Wilkie of Germany) pocket compass #24226—SD.

Left to Right (bottom row). (1) Silva Ranger—OR with declination adjustment. (2) Silva Type-3—OR. (3) Silva Huntsman—OR. (4) Suunto SP-68—OR. (5) Suunto RA-69DE—OR with declination adjustment.

ment unless you want sophisticated features like optical sights and a mechanical adjustment for declination (discussed in the sections which follow).

Floating Dial Compasses

These are the easiest to use. They have no dials to turn and you read the compass in the same plane as your objective. You merely point the instrument toward your destination and read the dial directly. There is nothing to set, and usually not even a cover to raise. If it is filled with liquid to slow the swing of the needle (damped), this model may be the fastest of all styles to use.

Cruiser Compasses

Cruiser compasses are almost identical to compasses used on surveyors' transits. Their basic design dates back many decades. Designed for use by professionals, cruisers come in solidly constructed aluminum cases and have long, free-swinging (undamped) needles. To use a cruiser, open the cover, hold the compass waist-high, and point the instrument at your objective. You read the dial where it is intersected by the north end of the magnetic needle (number graduations are reversed to permit reading the compass in this fashion). All cruisers have an internal means for offsetting local magnetic declination. Most compasses of this style are very heavy (8 ounces or so), cumbersome, and slow to use. Few are really waterproof, and none are usable at night. They are very expensive. Although quite accurate, there are better styles for the canoeist.

Fixed Dial Compasses

The stationary or fixed dial compass has for years been the traditional route-finding instrument of the wilderness traveler. The design of these instruments dates back hundreds of years. Best typified by the gumball machine variety, they are still manufactured because most people just don't know how to use any other kind. These models are fine for playing at navigation but should be avoided for any kind of serious route finding.

Lensatic and Prismatic Compasses

These are floating dial compasses with sophisticated sighting devices. Unfortunately, most are not very good. Expensive models work well and are by far the most accurate hand compasses in production. The cheapies (under twenty dollars) generally have poorly aligned sights, rickity mounting systems, or sufficient parallax to prevent accurate sightings. Moreover, the lack of versatility of these compasses is a drawback (see "Orienteering Compasses").

Orienteering Compasses

The most versatile and suitable compass style for the canoeist is the orienteering model. Orienteering compasses have built-in protractors which allow you to quickly and accurately compute direction and scale distance from a map without first orienting the map to north. This means you can define a *precise* direction (to the nearest degree) while sitting in your bobbing canoe. Additionally, the direction is physically set on the compass by turning a dial. There is nothing to remember and nothing to write down.

Since all orienteering models are liquid-damped, finding the direction of travel once it has been determined from the map can be done quickly— generally within seven seconds. Orienteering compasses are very waterproof, light, compact, and unusually rugged. I once saw a jeep run over a Silva Ranger model. Although the cover was ruined, the compass was still usable for rough work. (When the instrument was returned to Silva for repairs a note of inquiry sent to the manufacturer was returned with the comment, "No charge—Silva compasses are indestructible!") To determine the bearing of an object with an orienteering compass, point the compass at the object, and while holding the base steady, rotate the graduated housing until the north end of the magnetic needle points to *N* (North) on the dial. The direction you are facing, in degrees, is locked onto the compass dial and can be read at an index inscribed on the base. The compass can then be slipped back into your pocket for reference later. And you don't have to remember the direction that was set on the compass, either, since it will remain positioned on the dial until you turn the housing. To verify your direction with this style of compass, merely point the instrument away from your body and rotate your body and the compass until the north end of the magnetic needle points to *N* on the dial.

Since you don't have to read the numbers set on the dial, orienteering compasses are ideal for use at night or under conditions of rain or poor visibility. A word of caution: do not leave liquid-filled compass in the sun. The expanding liquid can cause the capsule, to explode and render your compass worthless. Hence, avoid the common practice of taping the compass to a canoe thwart to provide instant readibility.

Although all high-quality compasses come with adequate instructions for average use, you should have an in-depth understanding of basic navigational principles if you intend to use your compass for serious route finding. There are many excellent books available dealing solely with navigation that should be consulted before undertaking a wilderness trip of much significance. At the end of this chapter there is a practice map you can use to test your route-finding ability. If you can successfully complete the map exercise, you are ready to set out on a wilderness trip on a reasonably complex waterway.

FIRST, THE BASICS

The compass is graduated in degrees. There are 360 degrees in the compass rose. The cardinal directions (north, south, east, and west) are each 90 degrees apart. The northeast (NE) quadrant encompasses the direction from 0 to 90 degrees, the southeast (SE) quadrant from 90 to 180 degrees, and so on. Learn to think in quadrants. Before determining the precise direction you wish to travel, ask yourself, "In which quadrant am I traveling?" This will help eliminate the most common of compass errors—the 180-degree error. For example, if your map tells you to go southwest and your compass points to 45 degrees (NE quadrant), you know something is wrong; you are facing 180 degrees in the wrong direction. It is not uncommon to transfer data from map to compass and make serious directional mistakes. A knowledge of your approximate direction of travel should be known *before* you get down to the specifics.

Using the map of Lost Lake at the end of the chapter (figure 48), assume you are at point *A*. You want to go just north of point *H* and take the portage trail to Hairy Arm. A glance at the map tells you to begin by heading northwest until you hit the shoreline, then to follow it around until you pass the bays leading into This Man's and That Man's Leg, then southwest into No Man's Leg and straight to the portage. Very

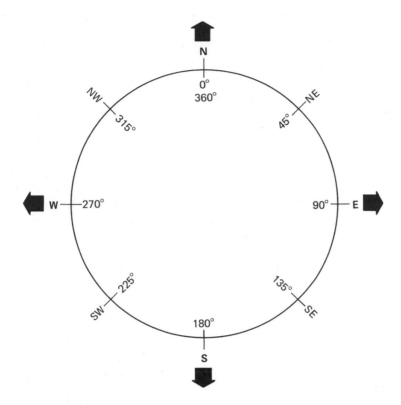

FIGURE 44. *The Compass Rose*

simple, right? Wrong! Look at the map scale. At 1 inch = 2 miles you won't be able to decipher islands from mainland or one bay from another. When you look out across a lake of this size and complexity you will see green as far as the eye can see. Physical features will blend with one another until the entire landscape is one of sameness. Because of wind and waves you will lose all sense of distance traveled. You can rely on your watch for a rough estimate, but it will be difficult for you to judge whether you have completed two miles or three. You can easily bypass No Man's Leg, or you can get turned around completely and become convinced that a channel between islands is a large bay, or vice versa. One of the greatest tragedies of twentieth-century canoeing occurred because of a map misinterpretation. In 1904 Leonidas Hubbard, Dillon Wallace, and George Elson attempted to penetrate the interior of an unexplored part of Labrador. "How vividly I saw it all again," said Wallace later on, "—Hubbard resting on his paddle and then rising up for a better view, as he said, 'Oh, that's just a bay and it isn't worthwhile to take the time to explore it. The river comes in here at the end of the lake. They all said it was at the end of the lake.' And we said, 'Yes, it is at the end of the lake; they all said so,' and went on." The Susan River they wrongly ascended was a dead end. With provisions gone and winter setting in, the expedition ended at Lake Michikamau, many miles from their destination. Hubbard, weakened by hunger and exhaustion, could not continue. He died on Sunday, October 18, 1904. His two companions, Elson and Wallace, retraced their fateful steps down the Susan Valley to civilization. We will never know why Hubbard, a man of experience, did not take the time to check his map and compass at such a critical point in his journey.

USING COMPASS AND MAP FOR PRECISION DIRECTION FINDING

In order to keep track of where you are on a body of water of any size, you must know, within reason, your position at all times. This means you can't just head in a general direction, you must proceed along an established direction, or *azimuth,* as it is called.

Assume you have begun a canoe trip at point *A* on Lost Lake (see the map of Lost Lake at the end of this chapter). You plan to paddle the full width of the lake and portage into the Hairy Arm of Found Lake, which lies just to the west. Horseshoe Island, you've heard, has an excellent campsite on its south end (point *B*), so you decide to make your first camp there. You choose to paddle straight to the campsite rather than take the longer, more confusing route around the shoreline to your west. To accomplish this you will need to determine the *exact* direction (azimuth) in degrees from point *A* (your location) to point *B* (your destination).

You can use your orienteering compass or a simple protractor for this computation. To use an orienteering compass, place either the left or right edge of the compass base plate on point *A*. Place the forward edge of the *same side* of the base plate on point *B*. Your compass is now pointing in the direction you want to go—from *A* to *B* (not from *B* to *A*). While holding the base plate tightly in position, turn the compass housing until north on the dial points to the top (north) of the map. Caution: don't use the magnetic needle! Your direction of travel—292 degrees—is now locked onto the dial and can be read at the index inscribed on the compass base. Now, while holding the compass in front of you with the direction-of-travel arrow inscribed on the base pointing *away* from your body, rotate your body and compass (you may have to turn the canoe to do this) until the magnetic needle points to north on the dial. You are now facing in the proper direction. Locate a notch or visible incongruity on the horizon that you can identify as being on this course of travel. Put your compass away and paddle toward your objective. Do *not* attempt to watch the compass needle and paddle at the same time! In time your objective (point *B*) will pop into view and you will have found your campsite.

Since precise directions are needed in canoe travel, the orienteering style compass has an obvious advantage over all other types. With a dial or cruiser model precise azimuth determination is possible only if you have a good protractor and sharp pencil at hand. And if that protractor should become lost or broken, accurate direction finding will be slow and time consuming at best.

Once you have reestablished your position at point *B*, you can continue your voyage to *C*, then to *D*, and so on. In this manner you can cross a large, complex waterway without fear of becoming lost, for you will know where you are all the time.

AIMING OFF

Assume you are at point *G* and you want to locate the portage to Hairy Arm just north of *H*. There are five portages leading out of No Man's Leg, but only one goes to Hairy Arm. Since one degree of compass error equals 92.2 feet per mile (tan. $1° \times 5280$ feet), even a slight error can be disastrous.

From *G* to the Hairy Arm portage is about three miles. A 4-degree error over this distance would cause you to miss the portage by at least 1100 feet, or nearly one-fourth of a mile. You would in effect be lost, since you would have no idea which direction to go to find the portage. Instead, *aim off*. Determine the azimuth from *G* to a point just north or south of the portage—in this case, point *H*, just south of your portage. Locate a notch on the horizon which corresponds to the azimuth you have computed, and start paddling. When you reach the shoreline, you will be somewhere near H, although you may be a few hundred feet north or south. But one thing is certain—you are *south* of the portage to Hairy

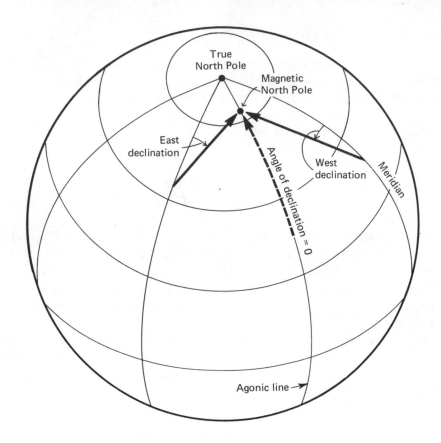

FIGURE 45. *Compass Declination—The Angular Difference between* True *North and* Magnetic *North* (*the direction the compass points*)

Arm. You merely have to paddle up the shoreline (north) until you come to the portage. This principle of aiming off is equally useful on land or for locating the mouth of a river. By aiming off you minimize the possibility of error.

DECLINATION

A compass points (actually, it doesn't point—it lines up with the earth's magnetic field) to *magnetic* north, not *true* north. This angular difference, called *declination*, must be considered whenever you use your compass (see figure 45). In the eastern United States the declination is westerly and in the western United States the declination is easterly. If you live right on the imaginary line which goes directly through both the true and magnetic north poles (called the *agonic* line), your declination will be zero.

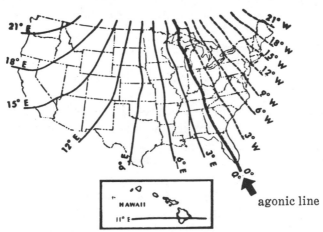

agonic line

FIGURE 46. *Standard Declination Chart*

If you live east or west of the agonic line, your compass will be in error, since the true north pole is not in the same place as the magnetic north pole. As you can see from the declination chart, the farther away you are from the agonic line, the greater the declination. Moreover, the magnetic north pole is constantly moving; because of this declination will vary from year to year as well as from place to place. Consequently, it is not possible for compass manufacturers to factory-adjust a compass to account for this variation. To find the exact declination for your area, consult a topographic map or call a surveyor. In the continental United States declination can range from 0 degrees at the agonic line to more than 20 degrees in New England and the far west. Unless your canoeing will be limited to those states very close to the agonic line, you will have to consider declination.

The easiest solution to the declination problem is to purchase a compass which has the mechanical means for offsetting this difference. Silva, Suunto, and Michaels of Oregon all make orienteering models with this optional feature, and all cruisers can be mechanically adjusted for declination. Prices for such compasses are generally in the fifteen-dollar-plus category; nevertheless, if you are a serious wilderness canoeist, the extra cost is worthwhile. If you are on a limited budget or live close to the agonic line, it is probably not necessary to purchase a compass with declination features. You may instead compute the variation mathematically, according to the following rhyme:

Declination east—compass least (subtract east declination from your map direction)
Declination west—compass best (add west declination to your map direction)

Maps are almost always drawn in their *true* perspective (any variation is so small that it can be ignored). So when you determine a direction of travel or azimuth from a map, it is a *true* azimuth. The true azimuth taken from your map will have to be converted to a *magnetic* azimuth to be set on your compass.

Assume a declination of 10 degrees east. Applying the rhyme "Declination east, compass least," *subtract* 10 degrees from the true azimuth computed from your map. In the Lost Lake map exercise a true azimuth of 292 degrees from *A* to *B* would equal 292 minus 10, or 282 degrees, using the declination given above. Conversely, if declination were 10 degrees west, it would be added (292° + 10° = 302°), and this value would be set on your compass. If this is confusing and you plan to travel in areas where the declination is large, you would be well advised to spend the extra money for a compass which can be manually adjusted for declination.

POSITION BY TRIANGULATION

Suppose you find yourself on a large, mazelike lake where you can identify two or more topographical features but you don't know exactly where you are. Finding your position by triangulation is simple with an orienteering compass (or you can use a protractor with a more conventional compass). Pick out one point on the horizon which you can identify—Old Baldy, in this case (see figure 47). With your compass, shoot a magnetic azimuth to the point (azimuth = 312 degrees). Change this magnetic azimuth to a *true* azimuth by reverse application of the rhyme: 312° + 6° = 318°. Draw the *back* (reciprocal) azimuth (318° − 180° = 138°) through Old Baldy, using your compass base plate and a sharp pencil. (When using an orienteering compass you don't have to compute

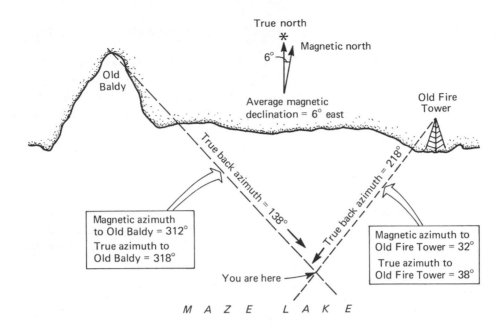

FIGURE 47. *Position of Triangulation*

the back azimuth at all.) Set 318° on the compass dial, place your pencil point on Old Baldy, and put the forward edge of one side of your compass base plate against the pencil point. Rotate the entire compass in an arc about the pencil until north on the *dial* (not the needle) points to the top (north) of the map. Caution: do not turn the compass housing during this operation, since the true azimuth which you just computed to Old Baldy (318°) is set on the dial. This procedure will *not* work if you change the dial setting! Using the base plate as a straight edge, draw your line. Repeat the exercise using another point on the horizon which you can identify (the old fire tower). You are located where the two lines cross. For greatest precision you may wish to take three sightings.

NAVIGATION AT NIGHT

Canoeing by moonlight on a slow-moving river or calm lake is an enjoyable experience. However, no canoeist's repertoire is complete until he or she has done some black-night travel by compass. Some years ago while canoeing in Minnesota's Boundary Waters Canoe Area, I was awakened to find three bears in camp—Mama and two babies. In spite of previous stern warnings, the youth group which I was guiding had left food scattered about the camp. The dehydrated fruit which was on the lunch menu evidently had a superabundance of prunes, and the youngsters had elected to have a prune fight. Even after a thorough policing of the grounds, enough prunes remained to attract the bears. We blew whistles, banged on canoes, clanked pots and pans, and made a variety of other noises in the hope of frightening away the hungry bruins; to no avail. Our bears were used to people. After they knocked down one tent we became convinced it was time to leave, and within a few minutes we put to sea. The night was black as pitch, but locating a new campsite without a moon to guide us was not difficult. We set course by compass and located a new site within an hour. My compass, a Silva Ranger, had a good luminous night sighting device.

If you travel at night it is important to obtain a compass with luminous points. A flashlight won't do, since the filament coil in a flashlight bulb functions as an electromagnet (and flashlights are made of steel, of course). Besides, navigating by flashlight requires continuous readjustment of your eyes to the light.

As to navigation by the stars, I know of no modern canoeist who has ever had to resort to such folly. If you are lost or without a compass, you have no business traveling at night, and if you do have a compass you certainly don't need the stars. Moreover, trees and topographical features sometimes prevent you from keeping the North Star in view. Such star navigation makes interesting reading for the armchair canoeist, but it is impractical and, on complex waterways, dangerous. If you are interested in this sort of thing, however, see a Boy Scout handbook or, for more detail, any text on surveying or astronomy.

YOUR WATCH AS A COMPASS

Although of questionable accuracy, direction finding using a watch is at times convenient when you want a rough, quick direction but you don't want to get your compass out. If your watch is correctly set for the time zone in which you are canoeing, you have merely to point the hour hand at the sun (keeping the watch horizontal). Halfway between the hour hand and twelve o'clock is roughly south. Such showmanship will impress your friends when things get dull on a long wilderness voyage (though Robert Owendorff pointed out the unreliability of this method in "How to Get Lost in One Simple Lesson," in the January 1973 issue of the *Izaak Walton League* magazine).

LOST LAKE EXERCISE

On page 172 is a map of Lost Lake (figure 48). Assume you are at point *A*. Using your compass or a protractor, determine the azimuth and approximate time of travel from point to point. Proceed alphabetically, ending your trip at the portage into Hairy Arm. Assume a travel speed of two miles per hour. When you have finished and your answers check, work the triangulation problem below.

TRIANGULATION PROBLEM

You can identify Dunker Hill at a magnetic azimuth of 256 degrees and Kaby Lookout at a magnetic azimuth of 4 degrees. Where are you located? Clue: don't forget to apply the declination.

ANSWERS TO LOST LAKE EXERCISE

Point	True Azimuth	Approximate Travel Time	Magnetic Azimuth (to be set on your compass)
A to B	290°	1¼ hours	284°
B to C	341	¾ hour	335
C to D	15	20 minutes	9
D to E	338	2 hours	332
E to F	274	1½ hours	268
F to G	244	½ hour	238
G to H	227	1¼–1½ hours	221

H to portage (paddle north up the shoreline to portage): time—about 15 minutes.

ANSWER TO TRIANGULATION PROBLEM

You are located at the north end of Horseshoe Island.

RIVER NAVIGATION AND TRIP GUIDES

No discussion of canoe route-finding would be complete without mentioning trip guides and river navigation. With the impact of man

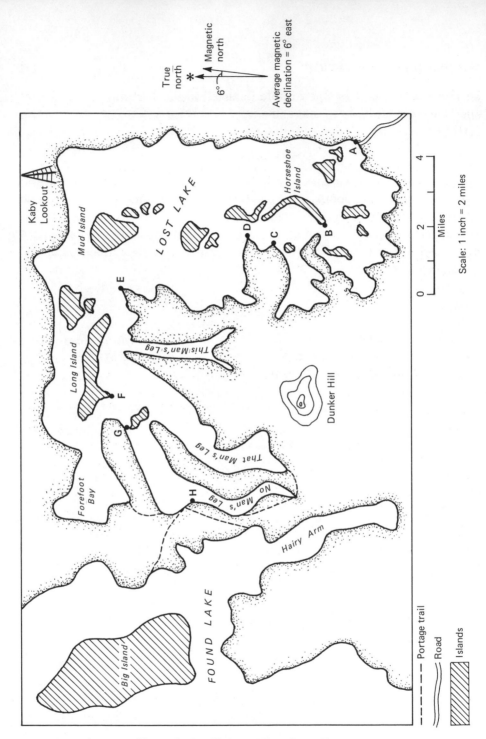

FIGURE 48. *Average Magnetic Declination Equals 6° East*

on river systems, it is becoming more and more important for the prospective river paddler to know what the water conditions are like before
setting the canoe in the water. Many local and even far northern rivers
are now dam controlled, and are very dangerous at high water or impossible at low water. Barbed wire fences strung across rivers maim and
kill canoeists each year, and the people who string these fences generally
have the law on their side. Each year we read about canoeists who inadvertently paddled over a dam because they didn't know it was there.
If you paddle rivers you must be able to accurately locate and identify
dams, rapids, fences, and other obstacles in the water which can endanger your trip.

Unlike lake navigation, it is very difficult to fix your position on a
river. A compass will be useful for rough directions only. You can re-
affirm your location at major river bends, identifiable rapids, or incoming streams. On wilderness canoe trips where it is necessary to ascend
an incoming stream and thereby change watersheds, a high degree of
resourcefulness and competency in map reading may be required, especially if there are many streams to confuse you. For trips on complex
waterways near the magnetic north pole (where compass pointings are
generally unreliable), a sextant or compact theodolite might be a wise
investment to insure navigational safety.

Lastly, some of the best maps of river conditions are the local people
who live in the area. Always check with them before embarking on a
river, even if you have run it many times. Many things may have
changed since your map was drawn. Although you should heed the advice
of local persons, bear in mind that most don't understand canoes. Locals
have a tendency to exaggerate the dangers of their rivers. Nevertheless,
they will provide you with much good information. Especially seek out
foresters or professional people who work in the area. Outdoors people
will generally tell it like it is, or at least they will exaggerate less.

12.
Food for the
Wilderness-Weary

The days of bean-hole and stew-pot cookery are gone. No longer must we sweat and choke over a hot, smoky fire to prepare something palatable. We can, instead, devote our energies to experiencing the joys of nature.

Anyone can prepare gourmet meals on wilderness trips these days. Everything from freeze-dried shrimp cocktail to Neapolitan ice cream can be purchased in packaged form from camping equipment shops. And you don't have to be an accomplished chef to prepare these foods, either; generally you need only boil water, add the product, and simmer for five minutes or so.

Fortunately for our pocketbooks, many of these lightweight, easy-to-prepare foods are commercially available in local supermarkets at substantial savings over the packaged stuff available from outfitters. And, interestingly enough, some of the food items, like soups, puddings, fruit drinks, and cake mixes, are equal to or better than similar products from equipment shop.

174

Although you can build considerable variety into a wilderness menu by combining the offerings of both supermarkets and equipment shops, sameness in food does not seem to bother most experienced outdoors people. In fact, some hearty wilderness travelers carry only beef jerky, dehydrated fruit, soup, oatmeal, and tea, and get along quite nicely for weeks at a time.

Anything goes on canoe trips of less than a week, and this includes large coolers filled with fresh hamburger, eggs, and, of course, beer. But for extended or white-water trips where weight must be carefully considered, only freeze-dried or dehydrated foods will do. If money is no object, you can merely pick 'em off the shelf of your local camping store. But if you're on a limited budget you can save tremendously by choosing grocery shelf products and repackaging them. Freeze-dried foods, although excellent for most canoe trips, don't supply enough calories (especially fat) for rugged, physically demanding voyages of several weeks. On rugged trips your body needs four thousand or more calories a day. These calories can be supplied by ample amounts of oatmeal, jam, cornbread, rice, peanut butter, margarine, and nuts.

MEAL MANAGEMENT

PACKAGING

Remove all excess packaging on foodstuffs (like cardboard boxes) and repack each meal separately in a large, heavy-duty plastic bag (Zip-Lock bags are ideal). Place plastic bags in color-coded nylon stuff sacks. If you pack all your breakfasts in a yellow nylon bag, your lunches in blue, and your suppers in green, you will avoid much pack groping at mealtime.

Each packaged meal should be a complete unit. It should not be necessary to search for the sugar, instant milk, cocoa, or whatever. All items should be premeasured in the correct amounts necessary to serve the group. Instant puddings, for example, call for the addition of milk. The correct amount of nonfat dry milk should be premeasured and added to the dry pudding mix in a plastic bag. Preparation of the pudding should require the addition of the correct volume of water only. If you premix all your foods in this fashion, you will shorten meal preparation time considerably.

A word of advice: when you repackage meals be sure to include the directions for cooking. I still have several bags of what-is-it-and-how-much-do-I-use? left over from previous canoe trips.

Save half-gallon milk cartons—lots of 'em. Pour one quart of water into each carton and put a line at the one-quart level. Now pack all your lunches in the milk cartons (after removing the water.)

Place crackers, candy bars, and strips of beef jerky in the cartons. The rigid containers will protect all your lunch breakables. Close the cartons, seal with tape, and place them in a plastic bag. Pack what won't fit in the cartons in the plastic bag. Seal the bag with a rubber band. Avoid twisties. They can puncture adjacent bags and end up strewn all over the landscape.

For lunch, use the empty milk cartons as measuring containers or save them for use as emergency fire starters.

Make an accessory bag (a large nylon stuff sack). Into this place toilet paper (plastic-bag each roll separately and crush thoroughly before placing in the bag), sugar, salt, pepper, and any special delight such as a package of mixed nuts. Bag items like cooking oil and pancake syrup separately in plastic even though these liquids come sturdily packed in nonleaking plastic bottles. A wilderness canoe trip is surprisingly rough on food and equipment.

HINTS

TO MIX MESSY PASTRY BATTERS

Pour batter and water into a plastic Zip-Lock bag. Seal the bag and knead the contents with your hands until they are well mixed. When the consistency is correct, punch a hole in the bag bottom and squeeze the mix (use the bag like a cake decorator) into your waiting oven. There is no mess, no fuss, and no washing of utensils. This is the best way to make Bisquick dumplings, which are dropped into boiling soup.

DRYING COOKWARE AND CLEANING EQUIPMENT

Package a half-dozen sheets of paper towels with breakfast and supper meals. The towels are handy for drying cookware, cleaning the stove, and similar chores.

CLEANING POTS AND PANS

If you have hangups about fire-blackened pots, soap each pot bottom with liquid soap or shaving cream before placing the pot on the fire. The bottoms will clean easily with a limited amount of elbow grease. Many experienced campers, however, consider black beautiful and dispense with this foolishness.

TO ASSURE SUFFICIENT SERVINGS OF FREEZE-DRIED FOOD

Virtually all manufacturers of freeze-dried foods are optimistic about the number of servings per package. For nonstrenuous recreational canoe trips increase each serving by one-fourth; for rugged wilderness ventures increase by one-third to one-half. Teenagers, especially, consume much more food on a wilderness trip than you might imagine. Unlike adults, who tend to foresee the consequences of their acts, youngsters often dip into the next day's till to satisfy their voracious appetites.

TO KEEP COOKED FOODSTUFFS WARM

When scrambled eggs, bacon, pancakes, or biscuits are the order of the day, keep these foodstuffs warm by placing them in a covered vessel set atop an uncovered, freshly brewed pot of coffee. Sufficient heat will be generated from the coffee to keep foods warm without the danger of burning. Additionally, your coffee will stay hot longer due to the added insulation of the extrathick pot top.

FOR THAT GOURMET TOUCH

To give added zest to virtually all dehydrated and freeze-dried entrees, include a small container of thyme and a fresh onion with your cooking gear. A small sliver of onion and a dash of thyme will turn mediocre mush into gourmet cuisine.

FOOD PROTECTION AND SANITATION

It has become increasingly difficult to find campsites along heavily traveled canoe routes which are devoid of litter, garbage, and human waste. Filthy campsites are more than just eyesores; they are health hazards. I have observed people deliberately scattering leftover food about the woods under the guise of feeding the animals, and I have watched people who should know better throwing the entrails of fish directly into the lake that provided their drinking water.

Misuse of natural areas is more often due to ignorance of basic ecological relationships than wanton abuse. For example, people don't always understand that it may take many months, or even years, for a small lake to completely flush itself clean of pollutants. Some over-crowded lakes may experience the paddles of more than ten thousand canoeists annually. If each dumps a single cup of leftover camp coffee or washes even a single pot in the water, the environmental impact upon the watershed will be severe. Nature has provided fish and wildlife with sufficient food of the proper kind to insure their health and well-being. The diet of wild creatures need not include man's garbage.

A few people are under the misguided impression that wild animals in isolated areas are dangerous. Such persons, for fear of bodily injury, steer clear of the deep woods. They feel that the presence of a fellow camper a few hundred feet down the lake will keep away the wolves, bears, mountain lions, and other potentially dangerous animals. In prac-tice, quite the opposite is true. A whole new breed of wildlife seems to be evolving—a breed that has become fond of, if not dependent upon, people's waste. The camp bear and garbage-can raccoon are distin-guished members of this new group. A camp bear, for example, who has been unwittingly fed by environmentally unaware campers, may become downright nasty when you attempt to shoo it away from your food pack with conventional means like whistles, yells, and the clank of pots and pans. Camp bears have destroyed entire campsites in their frenzied searches for food. Like humans, animals know a good thing when they see it, and once they find a free meal they're sure to return for another. The number of rampaging bears killed by forest and park personnel has increased substantially from that of a generation ago. The fault is ours. A clean camp area and a well-protected food supply are the main in-gredients in a pleasant and event-free canoe trip.

FOOD PROTECTION

Before you retire for the night, your food supply should be carefully sealed in plastic and secured in your Duluth pack. If there is any evidence that a bear or raccoon has recently frequented the area, the pack should be treed. Tie one end of your 50-foot rope through the pack straps and throw the free end, weighted with a rock, over a tree limb at least 15 feet above the ground. Haul the pack up to the limb and secure the rope around the tree trunk. Your small nylon pulley, if you have one, is useful here, for care must be taken not to get the hauling rope caught in the tree bark. This can be a problem because the weight of the heavy food pack will cause the rope to bite deeply into the wood. I once got a rope so tightly wedged in a tree limb that it required an hour's effort to get the treed pack down.

To prevent a bear from climbing the tree and grabbing the food, some canoeists suspend the pack from a pole placed between two nearby trees. I don't feel this additional precaution is necessary, however, since the bear won't find the food if he can't smell it, and usually if the pack is well up in the air the wind currents won't bring food odors down to the ground.

Possibly the best clue to the existence of a camp bear is the condition of the campsite. If the area is a genuine mess, perhaps with tiny scraps of paper scattered about, suspect animals immediately. Even sloppy campers don't purposely throw garbage everywhere.

Unless there is evidence of marauding animals, I seldom tree my food packs (I confess to laziness . . . and late-night popcorn-brandy parties). Except for my experience with the three bears mentioned earlier, I have never had animal trouble. But I am *very* careful with my food.

Grounded food packs should be placed well away from the immediate camp area, and under no circumstance should you keep food in your tent. An experienced camp bear will casually destroy anything in his way—even you—to get at food. Almost without exception, bear maulings can be traced to careless food habits.

Some canoeists rig a night alarm system by placing pots and pans atop their grounded food packs. The idea here is that a hungry bear or coon will knock the cookwear down, creating sufficient racket to awaken the sleeping campers.

Occasionally canoeists place their food packs beneath their canoes in the hope that this will deter a determined bear. This I consider downright dangerous—to the canoe, that is. Bears are extremely powerful animals, and they can easily smash a canoe with a friendly swipe of a paw.

Before you become convinced that the woods are filled with enraged wild animals, let me again emphasize that in the thousands of miles I have traveled by foot and canoe, I have had bear-trouble only once. The woods are considerably safer than city streets.

SANITARY DISPOSAL

For short trips where there are few portages, all garbage should be bagged in plastic and packed out of the wilderness. When this is impractical, as on lengthy outings, the best and most widely accepted method of disposal is burning. Before burning uneaten food, build a good, hot fire so that the remains of soupy foodstuffs won't extinguish the blaze. Burn all garbage *completely*, being sure to pick aluminum foil out of the flames before it melts all over everything. Partially melted and fire-flaked aluminum foil is rapidly becoming the scourge of the wilderness. Cans and bottles have been outlawed in many areas because people refused to pack them out. Soon aluminum foil may also be outlawed.

Disposing of fish entrails can be a problem. If you throw them in the lake, you pollute the water, and if you toss them back in the woods, they attract wild animals. What then is the best solution?

If you are in an area where sea gulls are prevalent (as in much of the northern lake country), place fish innards on a large boulder well away from human habitation. Within an hour the remains will be devoured by gulls, and since fish is the natural food of these great birds, you will have done little to upset their ecology.

Where no sea gulls can be found, the most satisfactory means of getting rid of viscera is by burying them. Bury fish remains as far away from the camp area as is practical, and cover them with eight to twelve inches of soil. This depth is best for decomposition and also minimizes the possibility of their being dug up by animals. Where there is only an inch or two of soil cover, as on the Precambrian geologic shield of Canada, place a heavy rock or log atop the buried entrails to hold them in place.

If possible, human waste, too, should be buried eight to twelve inches deep. Toilet paper and sanitary napkins should be burned. Just light the paper where it is, and when the flames are extinguished, cover with soil. Human refuse decomposes quickly, but paper products, unless burned, will remain an eyesore for at least a complete season, maybe more.

Dishes (or anything else) should be washed on the land, well away from the water's edge. Greasy dishwater is best poured into a small hole in the ground and covered with a few inches of soil. And it should go without saying that detergents should be biodegradable and phosphate-free. Better yet, avoid detergents entirely and boil your dishes clean. A little grease on your bowl won't hurt you—as long as the grease is yours. For this reason you should never use the eating gear of another member of your group. This simple precaution will eliminate minor illnesses.

The wilderness canoeist achieves a closeness to the land and water that can be gained by no other method of travel. The paddler views nature in all its unspoiled beauty, as a panorama unfolding before his or her eyes. But man's indifference to nature has muddied the crystal waters of the wilderness. Only a knowledgeable and caring generation can restore their clarity.

13.
The Wet-
Weather Fire

Contrary to popular belief, fire building is not easy—especially under inclement conditions. If it has rained steadily for several days or weeks, even an experienced, woods-wise person will have difficulty turning the flicker of a match into a roaring blaze. I remember a canoe trip that I took into the Boundary Waters Canoe Area of Minnesota early one spring. The ground, drenched with the rain of many weeks, yielded only the wettest of wood for fuel. To start a fire under those conditions required at least thirty minutes, a candle stub, some balsam pitch, a few dead cedar boughs, and a goodly supply of kindling cut from sticks robbed from a beaver house.

Unfortunately there is no "right way" to build a fire. What works under one set of circumstances may fail miserably under another. Nevertheless, some fire-building methods always seem to produce more positive results than others. For me, at least, the procedure described below has proved nearly faultless under the most difficult climatic conditions.

BUILDING THE FIRE

TINDER FIRST

A fire begins when a match ignites some very flammable material, called *tinder*. Perhaps the best way to get dry tinder when the woods are wet is to split the driest log you can find and then cut long, thin shavings from the split pieces of heart wood with your knife. The key to making good, long shavings, as opposed to short, broken ones, is to move your knife blade back and forth in a sawing motion while applying only moderate pressure. Even a very dull knife will produce usable shavings if a sawing rather than whittling motion is used.

If you are tripping in the north woods where the balsam fir is a common tree, simply break some resin blisters on the sides of the tree with a sharp stick or your knife tip and let the liquid pitch run onto your shavings. If you treat several shavings in this manner, you will have primed them with a fluid nearly as flammable as kerosine.

Cedar bark and cedar branches, even when they are green, ignite very fast into a hot, bright flame, and these, too, can be used for tinder if they are available.

Squaw-wood, the tiny dead lower tree branches which are no larger in diameter than your little finger, usually make superb wet-weather tinder, especially if shavings are taken with a pocket knife. Due to the protective cover of tree canopies, squaw-wood will remain relatively dry even after many days of rain. If it is sufficiently dry squaw-wood will break cleanly between your fingers with a loud, crisp snap.

Birch bark, too, is excellent, but for environmental reasons please don't strip the bark from living trees. Often you can find a very dry piece of birch bark hanging below a downed tree or log. Don't use bark or wood which has been in contact with the ground for some time, however, as it is most likely rotten, and rotten wood won't burn.

Abandoned birds' and hornets' nests and thin strips of bark peeled from grape vines also make good tinder. So, too, does Kleenex, and—in an emergency—dollar bills. Wood robbed from a beaver house is excellent, since it is very tough and dry, and when it is burned it produces a hot, nearly smoke-free flame. Again, for environmental reasons please don't rob beaver houses, except in dire emergencies—and even then take only a few sticks.

Leaves and grass have poor heat output and tend to suffocate a fire.

Using leaves for tinder marks you as a tenderfoot—that is, if your fire won't start.

During wet weather I first look for dry birch bark, and if this is unavailable I search for large diameter (one-half inch or so) squaw-wood and take shavings with my pocket knife. If dry tinder cannot be secured by this method, I split the driest log I can find and obtain shavings from the splittings, as mentioned earlier.

CONSTRUCTION

Obtain a pair of similar-sized logs about ½ inches in diameter and position them about 6 inches apart. Place 3 pieces of kindling (large-diameter squaw-wood or splittings) at right angles across the logs about one inch apart.

Stack shavings (tinder) on top of the kindling to a height of perhaps 1 inch. Take care to "scientifically" place each shaving. A common mistake is just to throw the tinder on the kindling supports. Fires often fail due to insufficient oxygen, so position each shaving carefully to provide plenty of air space.

Next, put two sticks about 1 inch in diameter over the ends of the logs at right angles to the fire base. These sticks will support the heavier kindling which you will pile atop the shavings.

Systematically criss-cross two or three tiers of fine split kindling above the tinder box. Don't place too much wood on the fire—excess wood will draw heat from the young flame, and to start wet wood you need all the heat you can get.

Your fire is now ready for lighting. Note that the tinder box sits on a platform a few inches off the ground. There are three reasons for the platform. First, cold, damp ground will rob the fire of much of its heat during the early stages of combustion. Second, the platform permits a continuous draft, similar to that of a hibachi grill. When you make a fire in wet weather you are already fighting one variable—wet wood. The raised platform eliminates a second variable—lack of sufficient oxygen. Third, hibachi-type fires provide ample room to place a match directly *under* the flammable tinder, which ground fires don't. When you light a hibachi fire, the heat goes upward—through the tinder—and is quickly transmitted to the kindling above by the straight-through draft of the raised platform. The tinder box of a typical ground fire, on the other hand, is often awkward to reach, and as a result only the very edge of the tinder is usually lit. The young fire, then, must burn sideways to ignite the rest of the tinder. As everybody knows, heat goes upward, not sideways! If the platform has a major fault, it is its susceptibility to wind. By building a low, well-shielded platform, however, this problem can be eliminated.

LIGHTING THE FIRE

Not long ago I watched two teenagers attempt to start a perfectly built platform fire. The youngsters used fifteen matches, quit in disgust, and called me. Without touching a single piece of wood, I lit the fire with one match. As the kids looked on in awe, I explained that my magic personality was responsible for the flame. "My smile," I said, "radiated heat!" In reality, of course, I knew where to place the match; the youngsters didn't. Improper placement of the match is a major reason why well-built fires won't start. You must know *where* to put the match before you put it there. Confused? Look at it this way. A match produces its best heat immediately upon lighting. The more of this initial heat you can trap, the better are your chances of starting the fire. So practice with an unlit match. Be sure the match head can be placed directly beneath the driest, most flammable tinder; rearrange your fire to accomplish this if necessary. Too often the fire-builder lights the match before deciding where to place it. By the time the decision is made, the match has either lost much of its heat or the wind has blown it out.

Once you have found a suitable place beneath the tinder where the match can be held, you are ready to proceed to the lighting of the fire. Strike the match as close to the fire as possible, and quickly touch the first flicker of flame to the tinder. Hold the match stick as long as possible, then drop it. Don't pull the match back out of the fire; you will lose too much heat if you do.

Outdoors books would have you believe that a rugged northwoods guide can get a fire going within a minute or two under any conditions. This is hogwash. Even the most experienced woodspeople occasionally "cheat" by using candles, fire starters, paper, and, yes—gasoline. Firebuilding is a simple skill that is easily learned, but there is no magic involved. Although the rather elaborate procedure described in this chapter may seem like a lot of needless work and fuss, it always produces good results—with a *single* match—at those miserable times when you need a fire most.

HINTS

I have found it best not to waterproof matches; instead, I prefer to carry them in a waterproof plastic bottle with a screw-on lid. I place a wad of cotton beneath the lid of the bottle to prevent scoring of the match heads. Although there are commercially waterproofed matches available, I am skeptical of their performance, especially when they are stored for several months or years. Waterproof matches, I have found, don't light as efficiently as nonwaterproofed ones; the waterproof coating tends to smother the flame. If, however, you want to waterproof your matches anyway, the best method I have found is to coat each match individually with nail polish or lacquer. I don't like to dip matches in paraffin as is sometimes recommended; paraffin-treated matches are almost always difficult to light.

A suitable watertight match case can be made from a pair of shotgun shells. Stack matches into an empty 16-gauge shell and slide a fired 12-gauge case over the smaller shell for a cover. The dead primers of the shell casings provide a convenient striker for the matches. Several of these simple match cases can be scattered in different packs to provide an emergency match supply.

Always carry a candle. Candles are necessary to provide the sustained heat required to ignite wet wood. Include a small birthday candle in your waterproof match case.

An effective method of drying wet matches is to draw them briskly through your hair. Don't use your clothes, though; they are much too abrasive.

Before you dismiss fire-building as an unnecessary skill, you should realize that it is not uncommon for people who are lost to use their entire match supplies and fail to start a fire. Your comfort and safety on a wilderness canoe trip depends upon the penny match and your ability to use it.

EXTINGUISHING THE FIRE

As a forester with the U.S. Forest Service some years ago I fought a twenty-acre fire in some scrubby alpine fir. The timber, I recall, was evaluated at about two thousand dollars, but the cost of extinguishing the blaze came to nearly one hundred thousand dollars. The fire was traced to a careless sheepherder, who was presented with the bill.

Most people don't realize that they are financially responsible for any forest fire they cause. This fact should not be taken lightly, for as the case in point illustrates, the expense involved in bringing even a small blaze under control can be exorbitant.

It should go without saying that your fire should be *dead out* when you break camp. In canoe country water is never a problem, and generous amounts of it should be used. Much of the canoe country of Minnesota, Canada, and Maine is rocky and has only a few inches of soil cover. To survive the high winds and rugged climate of the far north, trees form a shallow, far-spreading network of roots which extend many feet in all directions. Root systems of neighboring trees intertwine and provide stability for the struggling vegetation. Combined with a thin surface layer of highly flammable duff, this subterranean web of life provides an ideal pathway for the underground spread of fire. A fire may smolder in the soil for hours, or even days, and travel many hundreds of feet along these roots to flame up where oxygen and fuel is again abundant.

For this reason it is best to check the remains of a fire by touching your fingers to the ashes and charred wood. If the remains are hot enough to burn your fingers, they are hot enough to burn a forest.

14.
Trip Planning and Transportation

TRIP PLANNING

I always reserve the first weekend in May for my annual white-water trip down the infamous Hell's Gate section of Minnesota's Kettle River. At this time of the year, Hell's Gate usually rates a high Class II or low Class III on the river rating scale—an exciting run in an open canoe, and reasonably safe if you're properly prepared.

I prepare extensively for any canoe trip which includes rapids of Class III or greater difficulty. In early May this means a wet suit, a helmet, an extra paddle, fifty feet of throwing line, a waterproof first-aid kit, a knife, and a giant truck innertube for additional flotation.

On one particular Kettle River trip I was, to my chagrin, over-prepared. This became apparent in the parking area near the point of departure. I was gingerly placing one foot into a leg of my wet suit when a smiling canoeist strode up. "Whatcha gonna use the wet suit for?" he asked. "The water temperature's only seventy degrees. The river's way down—she won't even go a good Class I today. I just *walked* through the first pitch! That innertube is a great idea, though. Why don't you leave the canoe on the car and ride the tube down through the riffles?"

I responded with a mumbled comment about an ounce of prevention and hastily threw the gear back into the car. I spent the remainder of the day swimming and tubing the rapids.

Although you can overprepare for a canoe outing, the fact remains that good planning is the main ingredient in a safe canoe trip.

If you always paddle with an experienced group or club, you won't have to worry about trip planning for the job will be done for you. If you show up for a canoe trip inadequately prepared, the trip leader will most likely either help you get properly prepared or will ask you to shuttle cars instead of paddle. Thousands of canoeists take canoe trips each year for which they are completely unprepared. Often trip planning does not even consist of the most elementary basic—consulting a map of the river before embarking. Most of these happy-go-lucky paddlers survive their ventures, and many enjoy themselves immensely. Often they repeat the same mistakes over and over again with no apparent bad effects. But a few unlucky canoeists damage their equipment, their boats, and their bodies. A very small number never lives to take another canoe trip.

You can get away with a good deal of haphazard planning if your trips will be taken on nonviolent waterways close to civilization under carefully calculated climatic conditions. However, to embark on a difficult wilderness venture without the most detailed preparation is to invite disaster. If the trip will be taken in an isolated area where emergency help is generally unavailable, planning should begin as early as possible— preferably nine months or more in advance of the date of embarkation. This will allow ample time to secure maps, trip guides, food, and special equipment.

To insure a successful expedition, the following procedure and timetable is recommended:

PLANNING SCHEDULE FOR A HYPOTHETICAL CANOE EXPEDITION
INTO ISOLATED AREA

TRIP DATES: *June 10 to July 10*

Timetable

SEPTEMBER OF THE PREVIOUS YEAR. Hold an organizational meeting of those who will be going on the trip.

1. Discuss, in a general fashion only, the trip you plan to take. Since maps will probably be unavailable at this early date, do some rough planning using road or county maps.

2. Decide the purpose of the trip; for example, canoeing to reach a destination, leisurely paddling and fishing, or strictly fishing. Many trips have been spoiled because a few members wanted to go fishing while others wanted to paddle. All trippers must be in complete agreement as to the purpose of the trip.

3. Select a trip leader. There must be one person who will take the major share of responsibility for the organization and preparation of the journey. Obviously the leader should be the most experienced member of the group.

The trip leader should assign responsibility to group members as follows (for small groups, double up jobs):

Select a navigator, who will write for maps and trip guides (see Appendix A for sources), obtain permits, and so forth. The navigator should have an interest in route finding and a nose for research, and should round up all sources of information which pertain to the proposed trip.

Select a public relations chairperson. This individual should contact the chamber of commerce nearest the jump-off point in an attempt to locate a pen pal who is familiar with the waterway you intend to travel. When a pen pal is found, explain your trip and request information regarding its feasibility. Be sure to ask for weather information and river difficulty ratings. Also, ask your contact person how long he or she thinks it will take you to complete your voyage. When you receive this information, allow at least fifteen percent additional time for the unexpected. As explained in Chapter 11 (Wilderness Navigation), maps go out of date quickly and rivers can fluctuate greatly from week to week. Your river may be still in flood stage in early June, while by mid-August it may be too low for good canoeing. Unfortunately, neither your map nor your trip guide will indicate this. For these reasons it is unwise to undertake a major canoe expedition without corresponding with a person who is familiar with the local water conditions.

One individual should develop a rough menu for the group's consideration at a later meeting.

Select a quartermaster (usually the trip leader). The quartermaster should develop a complete equipment list, including group items, (like tents and canoes) and an individual checklist.

The most experienced paddler of the group should undertake the responsibility of being training chairperson. At least two short check-trips should be taken by the group before embarking on the big adventure. Ideally, one trip should be a day session to concentrate on the mastery of white-water technique and to find out which group members are best matched as paddling partners. A second trip should be an overnight affair. Test your equipment, your menu, and your rapport with other group members on this trip.

NOVEMBER OF THE PREVIOUS YEAR. Hold your second organizational meeting. It sometimes takes a month or more to obtain topographic maps in the scale you want. You may by this date still not have all your maps and trip guides, but enough should be on hand to begin planning in earnest. Attempt to accomplish the following at this meeting:

1. Go over the equipment checklist item by item. Be overprepared! Decide who will furnish the major items of equipment, like tents, canoes, stove, cooking gear, and so on.

2. Make sure each individual has adequate personal gear. For example, you should not permit the use of cheap plastic rain suits, poor-quality sleeping bags, badly constructed paddles, or inadequate footwear. You can only move as fast and as comfortably as the slowest member of the party, and one person with shoddy equipment can spoil it for everyone.

I vividly remember the ten straight days of driving rain we had on a canoe trip to Moosonee, Ontario, in 1974. One member of our group did not have waterproof footgear. By the fifth day of the trip, his feet were so wet and cold that he could barely continue. Luckily someone had an extra pair of rubber boots. Our frigid-footed friend gratefully accepted the boots (which fortunately fit) and completed the trip in comfort.

3. It is important that each individual be thoroughly committed to going on the trip. You just can't afford to plan for several months, buy special equipment, and then have someone back out at the last moment. To make sure this doesn't happen, compute the approximate cost of the trip, divide by four, and set up a schedule of payments:

$25 due by January 1 (nonrefundable deposit to insure commitment)
One-quarter of the total cost due by February 15
Another quarter of the cost due by March 15
Third quarter of the cost due by April 15
The remainder of the cost due by May 1

It is essential that you have some working capital on hand in the early stages of the trip. If the trip is very long, you will have a sizable cash outlay for food, and much of this food will need to be advance-ordered from a camping shop or by mail. A common mistake is to wait too long to order food. Many camp shops and mail order houses have difficulty furnishing some food items after May 15.

4. Select a treasurer to handle incoming monies. The treasurer should prepare an account book which lists debits and expenditures made by members. The group can settle up in June.

5. Agree on a policy for the repair or replacement of damaged canoes and equipment. Most groups choose to split the cost evenly, regardless of who is at fault.

6. Arrange for the return to your starting point. If you are traveling by train, make sure you have up-to-date schedules. If you plan to fly back, find out what the charter pilot's restrictions are on transporting canoes and equipment. Some charter planes simply won't take canoes. If you will drive, who will shuttle your car(s)? These questions should be answered as early as possible in the planning stages of your trip.

JANUARY: third organizational meeting.

1. Collect commitment money. Perhaps imbibe some fine wine to celebrate!

2. Finalize the equipment list and order what you need.

3. Check on maps and trip guides. If you don't have everything yet, send out follow-up letters.

4. Finalize the menu to everyone's satisfaction. Decide what can be bought at the local supermarket and check items to be mail- or equipment-shop ordered.

FEBRUARY: fourth organizational meeting. Have a menu party. Order mail-order food items and prepare a list of foodstuffs to be presented to your grocer.

MARCH: fifth organizational meeting. Have a map party. Cut, paste, tape, and cover with clear contact paper all your maps and trip guides (each group member should have his or her own map set). Go over the maps and trip guides in detail and compare these with information received from your area contact person. Note any discrepancies among the materials. If information is lacking, now is the time to write (or phone) for it. You have only three months left until launch time!

APRIL: sixth organizational meeting. Spring has arrived; the excitement mounts!

1. Go over any correspondence you have received since the last meeting. Tie up loose ends and socialize. Convince your spouse you are really going!
2. Firm up training session dates.

FIRST WEEK IN MAY: seventh organizational meeting. The countdown begins! Have a food-packing party! Repackage food, make beef jerky, and so on.

SECOND WEEK IN MAY: last meeting before the trip!

1. Have an equipment-packing party. Pack all group and personal gear, except those items you will wear or carry. Be sure to use a checklist so you don't forget anything.
2. Relax and celebrate! I assume you have all survived the practice canoe trips, you like the food, you get along well with each other, you are competent paddlers, and you have the right equipment. Nine months of detailed planning and preparation have gone into your canoe expedition. You are now ready to give birth to a great adventure!

Transportation

Perhaps the most difficult part of organizing a canoe trip is securing the transportation back to your starting point. Most canoeists simply run an auto shuttle. Shuttles, however, necessitate the use of two cars, and often you have only one. This is a real problem, especially for groups or families who are traveling together in a single vehicle.

The most obvious way to solve the transportation dilemma is to pay a local person or commercial outfitter to drive your car to the end of your trip. If you can arrange to have your car shuttled at the leisure of the driver (while you are on the water) rather than at a specific time, the cost will be much less.

An increasingly popular means of getting back to the starting point is by bicycle. For short trips where you won't be carrying much gear, merely set the bicycle in the canoe (wheels up) and take off (under paddle power, of course) downstream. Granted, your rig will attract stares of wonder and you will be beseiged with wisecrack remarks, but you will have solved your transportation problem effectively. When your trip is completed your partner can watch the canoe and outfit while you peddle back to the car. Since most river shuttles are seldom more than twenty miles long (one way), you should be able to cover this distance easily in an hour and a half or so.

For long trips where you don't have room for a bike in the canoe, run your own shuttle by dropping off the two-wheeler at your take-out point. You can chain the bike to a tree, or if it is a valuable model, pay a local person a couple of dollars to keep it for you until you finish the trip.

Another good way to shuttle yourself back to your car is to hitch-hike. The important thing about hitchhiking, however, is to make sure you look like a canoeist rather than a bum, and after you've been out camping for several days it is frequently difficult to make the distinction. An often foolproof way to get a ride is to wear your life jacket and carry a paddle. Make sure oncoming motorists see the paddle and jacket and you usually won't have any trouble getting picked up. It is essential that you wait near a bridge or road close to the river, as your chances of getting a lift will decrease as your distance from the river increases. I have yet to wait more than twenty minutes for a ride in all the times I have hitchhiked. On several occasions sympathetic drivers took me right to my destination.

WHERE TO GO

Due to the impact of humans, wilderness waterways are changing so rapidly that it is impossible, or at least impractical, to give detailed descriptions of the best paddle routes. At this very moment there are canoeists who are planning trips into supposedly isolated areas, using outdated canoe books as their major source of information. Right now plans are underway to dam some of the finest canoeing waters in northern Canada; and in the United States the U.S. Army Corps of Engineers is continually channeling, straightening, and otherwise "improving" our rivers. As a result many exciting canoe trips of the past, as outlined in the literature, are nonexistent today. You will have to search diligently to find challenging waterways where you can be completely alone.

Surprisingly, some of your best wilderness canoeing will be on small, meandering streams and rivers close to home. Local rivers are often too shallow for good motorboating, too slow for white-water thrills, and too inaccessible by road for good fishing. Such "unexciting" waterways may be more wild than the majority of those described in fancy guide books.

I would caution any canoeist against undertaking a wilderness trip of significance on the strength of a guide book alone. Even trip guides distributed by government agencies are apt to be outdated and inaccurate, and many of the best topographic maps available are many years old.

The best wilderness canoe trips will not be found in how-to-canoe books or published guides. Wilderness canoeists are often solitary people, and when they find a beautiful, isolated route, the last thing they want to do is advertise it. A wilderness trip described in print is an invitation to a wilderness despoiled. A good example is the infamous Chattooga River in North Carolina. Prior to the making of the film *Deliverance,* no one had ever heard of the Chattooga. Today this river draws hundreds of white-water paddlers each season, many of whom come totally unprepared—both in equipment and paddle skill.

Because of my great love for the wilderness, I prefer to remain secretive regarding my private haunts. Consequently there are no favorite floats described in this book. I leave the discovery of the last remaining wilderness waterways to you.

Appendix A
Map Sources and
Canoeing Guidebooks

The U.S. Geological Survey is the most complete and least expensive source of topographic maps. Indexes to topographic maps for each of the fifty United States are available free from the Geological Survey. Maps can be ordered directly from the appropriate USGS office listed below, or can be purchased from one of the many private map dealers whose names and addresses appear in the indexes. Each state index also contains a complete listing of city libraries which carry USGS maps.

STATE TOPOGRAPHIC MAPS

To order maps of areas west of the Mississippi river, write to:

Branch of Distribution
U.S. Geological Survey
Federal Center
Denver, Colorado 80225

To order maps of areas east of the Mississippi river, write to:

> *Branch of Distribution*
> *U.S. Geological Survey*
> *1200 South Eads Street*
> *Arlington, Virginia 22202*

To order Canadian topographic maps, write to:

> *Map Distribution Office*
> *Department of Energy, Mines, and Resources*
> *615 Booth Street*
> *Ottawa, Ontario*
> *Canada K 1A OE9*

Each Canadian province has a clearinghouse for provincial and county maps and legal surveys. Canoe routes and trip guides are sometimes available. Inquiries should be specific.

> *Director, Technical Division*
> *Department of Lands and Forests*
> *Natural Resources Building*
> *Edmonton, Alberta*

> *Director of Surveys and Mappings*
> *Department of Lands, Forests, and Water Resources*
> *Parliament Building*
> *Victoria, British Columbia*

> *Director of Surveys*
> *Department of Mines and Natural Resources*
> *Winnipeg, Manitoba*

> *Department of Lands and Mines*
> *Fredericton, New Brunswick*

> *Director of Crown Lands and Administration*
> *Department of Mines, Agriculture and Resources*
> *Confederation Building*
> *St. John's, Newfoundland*

> *Department of Mines*
> *Halifax, Nova Scotia*

> *Surveys and Engineering Division*
> *Department of Lands and Forests*
> *Toronto, Ontario*

> *Department of the Environment and Tourism*
> *Map Library*
> *P.O. Box 2000*
> *Charlottetown, Prince Edward Island*

Surveys Branch
Department of Lands and Forests
Quebec City, Quebec

Controller of Surveys
Lands and Surveys Branch
Department of Natural Resources
1739 Cornwall Building
Regina, Saskatchewan

STATE GEOLOGICAL SURVEYS

Every state has a geological survey office, and this is a good place to get up-to-date topographic maps. Although you can obtain identical maps from the U.S. Geological Survey at slightly less cost, your state will usually process orders faster (it is not uncommon to wait two or three weeks for U.S. Geological Survey maps, while state geological survey offices generally ship maps within a few days after the request is received).

Geological Survey of Alabama
P.O. Box Drawer O
University of Alabama
University, Alabama 35486

Department of Natural Resources
3001 Porcupine Drive
Anchorage, Alaska 99504

Arizona Bureau of Mines
University of Arizona
Tuscon, Arizona 85721

Arkansas Geological Commission
State Capitol Building
Little Rock, Arkansas 72201

Division of Mines and Geology
Department of Conservation
P.O. Box 2980
Sacramento, California 95814

Colorado Geological Survey
254 Columbine Building
1845 Sherman Street
Denver, Colorado 80203

Connecticut Geological and Natural History Survey
Box 128, Wesleyan Station
Middletown, Connecticut 06457

Delaware Geological Survey
University of Delaware
16 Robinson Hall
Newark, New Jersey 19711

Department of Natural Resources, Bureau of Geology
P.O. Box 631
Tallahassee, Florida 32302

Department of Mines, Mining, and Geology
19 Hunter Street S.W.
Atlanta, Georgia 30334

Division of Water and Land Development
Department of Land and Natural Resources
P.O. Box 373
Honolulu, Hawaii 96809

Idaho Bureau of Mines and Geology
Moscow, Idaho 83843

Illinois Geological Survey
121 Natural Resources Building
Urbana, Illinois 61801

Department of Natural Resources
Geological Survey
611 North Walnut Grove
Bloomington, Indiana 47401

Iowa Geological Survey
16 West Jefferson Street
Iowa City, Iowa 52240

State Geological Survey of Kansas
University of Kansas
Lawrence, Kansas 66044

Kentucky Geological Survey
University of Kentucky
307 Mineral Industries Building
120 Graham Ave.
Lexington, Kentucky 40506

Louisiana Geological Survey
Box G, University Station
Baton Rouge, Louisiana 70803

Maine Geological Survey
State Office Building
Room 211
Augusta, Maine 04330

Maryland Geological Survey
214 Latrobe Hall
Johns Hopkins University
Baltimore, Maryland 21218

Massachusetts Department of Public Works
Research and Material Division
99 Worcester Street
Wellesley, Massachusetts 02181

Michigan Department of Natural Resources
Geological Survey Division
Stevens T. Mason Building
Lansing, Michigan 48926

Minnesota Geological Survey
University of Minnesota
1633 Eustis Street
Saint Paul, Minnesota 55108

Mississippi Geological Survey
Drawer 4915
Jackson, Mississippi 39216

Division of Geological Survey and Water Resources
P.O. Box 250
Rolla, Missouri 65401

Montana Bureau of Mines and Geology
Montana College of Mineral Science and Technology
Butte, Montana 59701

Nebraska Conservation and Survey Division
University of Nebraska
113 Nebraska Hall
Lincoln, Nebraska 68508

Nevada Bureau of Mines
University of Nevada
Reno, Nevada 89507

Geologic Branch, Department of Geology
James Hall, University of New Hampshire
Durham, New Hampshire 03824

New Jersey Bureau of Geology and Topography
John Fitch Plaza
P.O. Box 1889
Trenton, New Jersey 08625

New Mexico State Bureau of Mines and Mineral Resources
Campus Station
Socorro, New Mexico 87801

New York Geological Survey
New York State Education Building, Room 973
Albany, New York 12224

North Carolina Division of Mineral Resources
P.O. Box 27687
Raleigh, North Carolina 27611

North Dakota Geological Survey
University Station
Grand Forks, North Dakota 58202

Ohio Division of Geological Survey
1207 Grandview Avenue
Columbus, Ohio 43212

Oklahoma Geological Survey
University of Oklahoma
Norman, Oklahoma 73069

Oregon State Department of Geology and Mineral Industries
1069 State Office Building
1400 S.W. Fifth Avenue
Portland, Oregon 97201

Pennsylvania Bureau of Topographic and Geological Survey
Harrisburg, Pennsylvania 17120

Rhode Island has no Geological Survey

South Carolina Division of Geology
P.O. Box 927
Columbia, South Carolina 29202

South Dakota State Geological Survey
Science Center
University of South Dakota
Vermillion, South Dakota 57059

Tennessee Department of Conservation, Division of Geology
G-5 State Office Building
Nashville, Tennessee 37219

Texas Bureau of Economic Geology
University of Texas at Austin
Austin, Texas 78712

Utah Geological and Mineralogical Survey
103 Utah Geology Survey Building
University of Utah
Salt Lake City, Utah 84112

Vermont Geological Survey
University of Vermont
Burlington, Vermont 05401

Virginia Division of Mineral Resources
P.O. Box 3667
Charlottesville, Virginia 22903

Washington Division of Mines and Geology
P.O. Box 168
Olympia, Washington 98501

West Virginia Geological and Economic Survey
P.O. Box 879
Morgantown, West Virginia 26505

Wisconsin Geological and Natural History Survey
University of Wisconsin
1815 University Avenue
Madison, Wisconsin 53706

Geological Survey of Wyoming
P.O. Box 3008
University Station, University of Wyoming
Laramie, Wyoming 82070

OTHER GOVERNMENTAL AGENCIES

Maps of local waterways may be obtained from the U.S. Army Corps of Engineers. A few of their field offices are listed below:

U.S. Army Corps of Engineers
219 Dearborn Street
Chicago, Illinois 60604

U.S. Army Corps of Engineers
P.O. Box 59
Louisville, Kentucky 40201

U.S. Army Corps of Engineers
1217 U.S. Post Office and Custom House
180 East Kellog Boulevard
Saint Paul, Minnesota 55101

U.S. Army Corps of Engineers
111 East 16th Street
New York, New York 10003

U.S. Army Corps of Engineers
P.O. Box 17277
Foy Station
Los Angeles, California 90017

The U.S. Coast and Geodetic Survey has a large assortment of topographic maps, aerial photographs, and surveys. Write for a free index.

For Aerial Photographs:
Coast and Geodetic Survey
Rockville, Maryland 20852
Attn: Photogrammetry Div. C-141

For Topographic Maps
Coast and Geodetic Survey
Rockville, Maryland 20852
Attn: Map Information Service, C-513

PRIVATE MAP COMPANIES

Topographic maps supplied by private map companies are identical to those available from state and federal geological surveys, but cost $.50 to $1.00 more per map sheet. The main advantage of private map companies is convenience. In most cases the maps you need are in stock; there is no waiting for back-ordered editions. Also, prepackaged quadrangles covering common wilderness areas are often available. Master map indexes are unnecessary; you merely tell the map company what you want and they will ship.

Wilderness Sports
Eagle Valley, New York 10974
Wilderness Sports offers a variety of packaged map kits. The kits consist of all the maps you need to successfully navigate your way through most of America's wilderness areas, with very good coverage of Canadian rivers. Wilderness Sports also offers a variety of Silva orienteering compasses, as well as map books and aids. Write for their free catalogue; you won't be disappointed.

W. A. Fisher Co.
Box 1107
Virginia, Minnesota 55792
Fisher maps are designed exclusively for the canoeist who travels in the Boundary Waters Canoe Area of Minnesota and Canada. The maps are printed on waterproof paper and show portages, rapids, falls, and campsites. Although not as accurate as topographic maps, Fisher maps are more useful to canoeists as they are designed expressly to satisfy their needs. A complete trip-planning

book containing fifteen maps which cover the Superior-Quetico region is available from the Fisher Company.

Hudson Map Company
1506 Hennepin Avenue
Minneapolis, Minnesota 55414

A complete topographic map service for the state of Minnesota.

Appalachian Mountain Club
5 Joy Street
Boston, Massachusetts 02018

Although not a map company as such, the Appalachian Mountain Club does have a complete file of maps covering all the major canoe routes of New England.

CANOEING GUIDEBOOKS

CANOE TRAILS OF NORTH-CENTRAL WISCONSIN
Wisconsin Trails Magazine
P.O. Box 5650
Madison, Wisconsin 53705

A complete map series and commentary written especially for the canoeist, this book covers ten of the best canoeing rivers in north-central Wisconsin.

CANOEING THE WILD RIVERS OF NORTHWESTERN WISCONSIN
Northwest Wisconsin Canoe Trails, Inc.
Gordon, Wisconsin 54838

Map series and commentary covering seven of the most popular rivers in northwestern Wisconsin.

CANOE TRAILS OF NORTHEASTERN WISCONSIN
Wisconsin Trails Magazine
P.O. Box 5650
Madison, Wisconsin 53705

Map series and commentary covering seventeen popular northeastern Wisconsin rivers.

CANOE TRAILS IN THE WISCONSIN GREAT DIVIDE AREA
Great Divide Canoe Trails, Inc.
Post Office
Ashland, Wisconsin 54806

Map series covering the Bad, White, Montreal, and nearby river systems.

MINNESOTA VOYAGEUR TRAILS
Minnesota Department of Conservation
Division of Parks and Recreation
320 Centennial Building
Saint Paul, Minnesota 55101

Contains seventeen of the most popular canoeing rivers in Minnesota. Shows some county roads.

GUIDE TO WHITEWATER IN THE WISCONSIN AREA, by Andres Peekna
Hoofers Outing Club
University of Wisconsin
The Wisconsin Union, 800 Langdon Street
Madison, Wisconsin 53706
A guide to popular white-water streams in Wisconsin. All rapids are assigned
American Whitewater Affiliation ratings.

MISSOURI-OZARK WATERWAYS, by Oscar Hawksley
Missouri Conservation Commission
Jefferson City, Missouri 65101
Covers 2200 miles of mostly easy streams in this area.

A.M.C. NEW ENGLAND CANOEING GUIDE
The Appalachian Mountain Club
5 Joy Street
Boston, Massachusetts 02018
A comprehensive guidebook to the waterways of New England.

CANOEABLE WATERWAYS OF NEW YORK STATE, by Lawrence Grinnell
Pageant Press, Inc.
130 West 42nd Street
New York, New York 10036
A broad coverage of the rivers of New York State.

EXPLORING THE LITTLE RIVERS OF NEW JERSEY, by Margaret and James
Cawley
(Second Edition)
Rutgers University Press
New Brunswick, New Jersey 08900
A composite of slow-moving, pretty, backcountry rivers.

APPALACHIAN WATERS, VOL. 1 AND 2, by Walter F. Burmeister
Appalachian Books
Oakton, Virginia 22124
An excellent sampling of the rivers of the eastern United States. Volume 1
includes the Delaware River and its tributaries, and Volume 2 includes the
Hudson River and its tributaries. An accurate mile-by-mile description.

WHITEWATER; QUIETWATER, *A Complete Guide to the Wild Rivers of Wis-
consin, Upper Michigan, and Northeast Minnesota,* by Bob and Jody
Palzer.
Evergreen Paddleways
1416 21st Street
Two Rivers, Wisconsin 54241
A detailed description of more than 750 miles of wild river trips in Wisconsin,
upper Michigan, and northeast Minnesota. There are international river ratings

for all rapids as well as a complete discussion of white-water technique and safety. One of the best guide books available. A must for every Midwestern canoeist's library.

A WHITE WATER HANDBOOK FOR CANOE AND KAYAK, by John T. Urban.
Appalachian Mountain Club
5 Joy Street
Boston, Massachusetts 02108

BASIC RIVER CANOEING, by Robert McNair
American Camping Association, Inc.
Bradford Woods
Martinsville, Indiana 46151

Abbreviated guides to canoeable rivers and streams are often available from your state's department of natural resources and conservation.

Appendix B
Where
to Get 'Em

The companies listed below are those with which I have personally done business. The quality of equipment and service offered by these firms is strictly top-notch.

EQUIPMENT

L. L. Bean, Inc.
Freeport, Maine 04032
An uncommonly nice company which still does business in the old-world tradition. L. L. Bean is your best source of pack baskets, shoe-pacs, and canoeing footwear. The company handles the excellent Quick 'N Easy car-top carriers. Good selection of woolens and general backpacking gear. Free catalogue.

Recreational Equipment, Inc.
1525 11th Avenue
Seattle, Washington 98122
REI is a co-op. You pay two dollars to join and you receive a yearly dividend (about ten percent) on your purchases. Although the co-op specializes in backpacking-mountaineering equipment, they have a large selection of items of

interest to canoeists. Prices are usually considerably below that of competitive distributors. Service is very fast; generally you can expect to receive your orders within two weeks.

Cabela's, Inc.
P.O. Box 199
812 Thirteenth Avenue
Sidney, Nebraska 69162

Equipment handled by Cabela's ranges from excellent to fair. Prices, however, tend to be very low. Sometimes extraordinary buys are possible on good-quality gear. Free catalogue.

Eddie Bauer
1737 Airport Way South
Seattle, Washington 98134

Equipment handled by Eddie Bauer is strictly top quality, and prices are very high. Nevertheless, Bauer has some unique equipment which is difficult to obtain elsewhere, and the company's guarantee is perhaps the best in the business. Free catalogue.

Holubar
Box 7
Boulder, Colorado 80302

Holubar specializes in mountaineering accessories. Their down-filled products, especially sleeping bags, are impeccably fashioned and are among the best in the industry. They have some interesting tents and outerwear as well as a good selection of backpacking stoves and accessories. Free catalogue.

The Ski Hut
P.O. Box 309
1615 University Avenue
Berkeley, California 94701

The Ski Hut manufacturers Trailwise equipment. They carry superb down-filled sleeping bags and outerwear as well as a good selection of gasoline stoves, Sigg and other cookwear, and are a good source of quality life vests like Harishok, Seda, Stearns, and Watercraft. Free catalogue.

Duluth Tent and Awning Co., Inc.
1610 West Superior Street
Duluth, Minnesota 55806

The only really complete source of Duluth packs. Write for free brochure. Duluth Tent and Awning will send samples of material upon request and will make up any canvas products to order. Free catalogue.

Bendonn Co.
4920 Thomas Avenue South
Minneapolis, Minnesota 55410

Manufacturers of the unique Bendonn lightweight aluminum Dutch oven.

Sierra Designs
Fourth and Addison Streets
Berkeley, California 94710

Sierra Designs manufactured the first 60/40 (52 percent cotton/38 percent nylon) wind parka. The company is well known for its quality down-filled products, especially parkas. Sierra Designs has one of the best Tarp Tents around. Free catalogue.

Eastern Mountain Sports
1041 Commonwealth Avenue
Boston, Massachusetts 02215

EMS has one of the most interesting and educational catalogues available (cost—one dollar). The catalogue not only suggests what to buy, but tells you, in detail, how to use it. It is a good source of life vests, abbreviated wet suits, rain gear, Fiberfill II and Polarguard sleeping bags. They also sell EMS kits (precut clothing, sleeping bags, tents) which you sew.

Frostline Kits
Department C
452 Burbank
Broomfield, Colorado 80020

Frostline manufactures a complete line of precut clothing, sleeping bag, rain wear, and tent kits. Directions are easy to follow and a simple straight-stitch sewing machine is all that is required to build the most complicated kit. Finished items are equivalent to similar top-quality products costing up to 50 percent more. Free catalogue.

The Great World of Ecology Sports
P.O. Box 250
250 Farms Village Road
West Simsbury, Connecticut 06092

Great World handles a variety of equipment especially suited for canoe use. Items include fiberglass spray decks, yokes, paddles, waterproof bags, waterproof camera bags, and white ash setting poles for poling the canoe. Free catalogue.

Forestry Suppliers, Inc.
Box 8397/205 West Rankin Street
Jackson, Mississippi 39204

The best source of map aids (adhesive backing, clear plastic coverings, measuring devices, etc.) around. Their giant catalogue is free, and includes a wide assortment of compasses and surveying equipment, pocket knives, signal flares, sharpening stones, first-aid gear, ropes, outerwear, and much more.

A. C. Mackenzie Co.
P.O. Box 9301, Richmond Heights Station
Saint Louis, Missouri 63117

Best source of modern aluminum setting poles (for canoe poling) and related information.

Carikit, Division of Holubar Co.
Box 7
Boulder, Colorado 80302

A variety of precut clothing, sleeping bags, and tent kits with easy-to-follow directions. A top-quality product results, with savings up to 50 percent over equivalent-quality products.

Bishop's Ultimate Outdoor Equipment
6804 Millwood Road
Bethesda, Maryland 20034

Manufacturer of Bishop Ultimate and Packlite tents.

Eureka Tent, Inc.
Subsidiary of Johnson Diversified, Inc.
625 Conklin Road, P.O. Box 966
Binghamton, New York 13902

Manufacturers of the excellent Eureka Drawtite and Timberline tents—two of the best canoe tents around. You can also get a variety of tent fabrics from Eureka. Very reasonable tent prices plus some ingenious tent designs.

Gerry, Division of Outdoor Sports Industries, Inc.
5450 North Valley Highway
Denver, Colorado 80216

Gerry manufactures and distributes a wide variety of camping accessories which range from expedition-quality tents to a tiny one-burner stove which, purportedly, burns any liquid fuel. Gerry tents and sleeping bags have been widely copied, but in spite of this Gerry equipment is still some of the best around. You pay a little more for the Gerry label, but you get well-made, quality gear.

Voyageur Enterprises
P.O. Box 512
Shawnee Mission, Kansas 66201

Voyageur carries what are possibly the most efficient, reliable, and reasonably priced waterproof gear bags currently available. Voyageur Enterprises also carries a few canoe-kayak accessories and some backpacking gear.

Stearns Manufacturing Co.
Saint Cloud, Minnesota 56301

Stearns manufactures a complete and very excellent line of life jackets. Stearns jackets are well designed, and there are several models available which meet the needs of canoeists. Prices are very reasonable.

Appendix C
Canoe Makers

OPEN CANOES

KEY TO CONSTRUCTION MATERIALS

FG: fiberglass (many manufacturers will build canoes with Kevlar instead of fiberglass at additional cost)
Al: aluminum
WC: wood and canvas
WD: wood
ABS: ABS (acrylonitrile butadiene styrene) plastic
ROY: ROYALEX ABS
OC: other construction, such as plastic-wood, nylon-plastic, etc.

Aero-Nautical, Inc., Skimmar Boat Division (FG)
154 Prospect Street
Greenwich, Connecticut 06830

Alumacraft Boat Co., Inc. (Al)
315 West Saint Julien Street
Saint Peter, Minnesota 56082

American Fiber-Lite Incorporated (OC)
P.O. Box 67
Marion, Illinois 62959

Aqua Sports Canada, Ltd. (FG)
525 Champlain
Fabreville, Lavai
P.Q., Canada

Appleby Manufacturing Co., Inc. (Al)
P.O. Box 591
Lebanon, Missouri 65536

Baldwin Boat Co., Inc. (FG)
Department C
Orrington, Maine 04474

Bemidji Boat Co., Inc. (FG)
Highway 2 West
Bemidji, Minnesota 56601

Black River Plastics (FG)
Box 327A
Route 301 South
LaGrange, Ohio 44050

Blue Hole Canoe Co. (ROY)
Sunbright, Tennessee 37872

Boat Technology (OC)
310 Curtin Avenue
Pittsburgh, Pennsylvania 15210

Aluminum Boats and Canoes (Al)
Browning Marine Division
900 Cheasaning Street
St. Charles, Michigan 48665

Brownline Canoes and Kayaks (FG)
2539 Bitters Road
San Antonio, Texas 78217

Burley Falls Canoe Co., Inc. (WD)
Burley Falls
Ontario, Canada

Chestnut Canoe Co., Ltd. (WC, Al, FG)
P.O. Box 85
Fredericton, New Brunswick
Canada

Chicagoland Canoe Base, Inc. (FG)
4019 North Narragansett Avenue
Chicago, Illinois 60634

Custom Fiberglass Products, Inc. (FG)
P.O. Box 101, Industrial Park
Mount Juliet, Tennessee 37122

Dolphin Products, Inc. (FG)
Department C
Wabasha, Minnesota 55981

Easy Rider Co., Inc. (FG)
10013-Fifty-first Avenue S.W.
Seattle, Washington 98146

Green Mountain Outfitters, Inc. (FG, RX)
P.O. Box 66
Forest Dale, Vermont 05745

Grayling Canoes (FG)
1271 South Bannock Street
Denver, Colorado 80223

Great Canadian, Inc. (FG, Al, WC, WD)
45 Water Street
Worcester, Massachusetts 01604

Grumman Boats (Al)
Grumman Allied Industries, Inc.
Marathon, New York 13803

Bart Hauthaway (FG)
640 Boston Post Road
Weston, Massachusetts 02193

Hollowform, Inc. (OC)
6345 Variel Avenue
Woodland Hills, California 91364

Iliad, Inc. (FG, ROY)
170A Circuit Street
Norwell, Massachusetts 02061

Indian River Canoe Manfacturing Co., Inc. (FG)
1525 Kings Court
Titusville, Florida 32780

Jaco, Inc. (Al, FG)
P.O. Box 460
Middlebury, Indiana 46540

Jensen Racing Canoes (WD, FG)
Eugene Jensen
308 78th Avenue North
Minneapolis, Minnesota 55444

Johnson Lures, Limited (Al)
P.O. Box 274
Brockville, Ontario K6V 5V5
Canada

Lincoln Canoes, Inc. (FG)
Route 32-C
Waldoboro, Maine 04572

Lowe Industries (Al)
Interstate 44
Lebanon, Missouri 65536

Lund American, Inc. (Al)
New York Mills, Minnesota 56567

Mad River Canoe Company, Inc. (FG, ROY)
P.O. Box 363
Spring Hill
Waitsfield, Vermont 05673

Michi-Craft Corp. (Al)
19997 19 Mile Rd.
Big Rapids, Michigan 49307

Midwestern Fiberglass Products (FG)
Box 247, Breezy Acres
Winona, Minnesota 55987
(manufactures Jensen Racing Canoes in addition to their regular line)

Mohawk Manufacturing Company, Inc. (FG, ROY)
P.O. Box 668
Longwood, Florida 32750

Monark Boat Company, Inc. (Al)
P.O. Box 210
Monticello, Arkansas 71655

Moore Canoes, Inc. (FG)
P.O. Box 55342, 5235 Winthrop Avenue
Indianapolis, Indiana 46205

Native Cedar Canoes (WD)
Reckards Canoe Shop
Rockwood, Maine 04478

Nona Boats (FG)
977 West 19th Street
Costa Mesa, California 92627

Norcal Fabricators, Inc. (Al)
Box 250
Callander, Ontario POH 1HO
Canada

Northern Fiberglass Industries, Inc. (FG)
747 Payne Avenue
Saint Paul, Minnesota 55101

Old Town Canoe Co., Inc. (FG, ROY, WC, WD)
Old Town, Maine 04468

Pack 'n Paddle, Inc. (FG)
701 East Park
Libertyville, Illinois 60048

Pine Tree Canoes, Ltd. (OS)
Box 824
Orillia, Ontario
Canada L3V 6K8

Precision Fiberglass Parts, Inc. (FG)
P.O. Box 416
Port Campus #2
Hood River, Oregon 97031

Quapaw Canoe Co. (FG)
600 Newman Road
Miami, Oklahoma 74354

Rivers and Gilman Moulded Products, Inc. (FG, ROY)
Main Street
Hampden, Maine 04444

Sawyer Canoe Co., Inc. (FG)
234 South State Street
Oscoda. Michigan 48750

Sea Nymph Corp. (Al)
P.O. Box 298
Syracuse, Indiana 46567

Seacrest Marine Corp. (ABS)
P.O. Box 522
Clarke Neck Road
Washington, North Carolina 27889

Seminole Canoe and Boat Company, Inc. (FG)
Sanford Airport Building 77
P.O. Box 43
Sanford, Florida 32771

6-H Products, Limited (FG)
80 Hickson Avenue
Kingston, Ontario
Canada

Smoker-Craft (Al)
Smoker Lumber Co., Inc.
Box 65
New Paris, Indiana 46553

Sportspal, Inc. (Al)
Industrial Park Road
Johnston, Pennsylvania 15904

Stalek Canoes (WD)
Marlburg and Co.
16 E. Chase St.
Baltimore, Maryland 21202

Starcraft Co. (Al)
2703 College Avenue
Goshen, Indiana 46526

Stowe Canoe Co., Inc. (FG)
Stowe Vermont 05672

Sunspot Plastic, Inc. (OC)
743 Kennedy Road
Scarborough, Ontario MIK 2C7
Canada

Tomahawk, Inc. (Al)
P.O. Box 310, River Avenue
Parker, Pennsylvania 16049

Trailcraft, Inc. (FG and kits)
Box 60680
Concordia, Kansas 66901

Tremblay Canoes, Ltd. (OC)
P.O. Box 655
Felicien, P.Q.
Canada

Troy Canoes (FG)
Athens, Ontario
Canada

Voyageur Canoe Co., Ltd. (FG)
King Street
Milbrook, Ontario LOA 1GO
Canada

Whitewater West (FG)
727 South Thirty-third Street
Richmond, California 94804

Wilderness Boats, Inc. (WD)
Route 1, Box 101A
Carlton, Oregon 97111

Wonacott Canoes, Inc. (WD)
P.O. Box 1902
Wenatchee, Washington 98801

Appendix D
Paddle
Manufacturers

Blue Hole Canoe Co., Inc.
Sunbright, Tennessee 37872

A superb white-water paddle with a polyurethane foam–filled shaft of 6061-T6 aluminum. The blade is formed from extruded ABS sheeting, covered with co-extruded acrylic (Korad). The paddle shaft is neoprene covered to retain warmth and for paddling comfort.

Ketter Canoeing
101-Seventy-ninth Avenue North
Minneapolis, Minnesota 55444

Quality-built Cadorette paddles of laminated spruce and cedar are well finished, beautiful, and very light—a popular racing paddle. Several models are available.

Calpino Paddles
433 Saint Mary's Road
Winnipeg, Manitoba
Canada R2M 3K7

Calpino's polyurethane-coated paddles of spruce and cedar are lightweight and well finished.

Cannon Products, Inc.
2345 N.W. 8th Avenue
Faribault, Minnesota 55021

The cannon paddle has an aluminum shaft with ABS blade and grip, and is easily adjustable for length. It is a reasonably strong, lightweight paddle for rocky use, identical to Grumman's Masterlite paddle.

Carlisle Ausable Paddle Co.
110 State Street
P.O. Box 150
Grayling, Michigan 49738

This company makes a lightweight paddle with aluminum shaft and ABS blade and grip.

Raymond A. Dodge, Importer
1625 Broadway
Niles, Michigan 49120

Dodge carries several models of Clement paddles with pear or T-grips; they are very strong, lightweight, of laminated constructon, well liked by racers, and strong enough for tough white-water use.

Feather Brand Paddles
Caviness Woodworking Co., Inc.
P.O. Box 710
Calhoun City, Mississippi 38916

Feather Brand makes a variety of paddle styles. Their best models are very adequate for wilderness tripping and are attractively priced. Avoid inexpensive models, which are prone to breakage.

Great Canadian, Inc.
45 Water Street
Worcester, Massachusetts 01604

Great Canadian has nicely made paddles of laminated mahogany.

Grumman Boats
Grumman Allied Industries, Inc.
Marathon, New York 13803

Grumman handles some very nice lightweight ash paddles which are moderate in price. Grumman's Masterlite paddles are identical to Cannon Company models and are priced about the same.

Bart Hauthaway
640 Boston Post Road
Weston, Massachusetts 02193

Hauthaway has a very light paddle with nicely finished fir shaft and molded fiberglass blade, which is not strong enough for white water, but fine for casual paddling—a quality-built paddle.

Hurka Industries
1 Charles Street
Newbury Port, Massachusetts 01950
Top quality Kevlar paddles with oval shafts, T-grips, and metal tips. Hurka paddles have been used by major expeditions and are built to withstand the toughest of whitewater uses.

Iliad, Inc.
168 Circuit Street
Norwell, Massachusetts 02061
Top quality white-water paddles, with neoprene-covered aluminum shafts and pressure-molded fiberglass blades. They are perfectly balanced, and possibly the lightest synthetic paddles currently available. Iliad's are used by many top slalom canoe competitors.

Kober
Hyperform, 25 Industrial Park Road
Hingham, Massachusetts 02043
The Kober is a superb quality laminated paddle with reinforced metal tip and veneer covering, used by international slalom canoe competitors.

L. L. Bean, Inc.
Freeport, Maine 04032
L. L. Bean does not manufacture paddles. The company does, however, stock a very excellent lightweight, all-ash paddle, nearly identical to that sold by Old Town—a light and very strong paddle.

Nona Boats
977 West Nineteenth Street
Costa Mesa, California 92627
An excellent white-water paddle with fiberglass shaft and pressure-molded fiberglass blade, the Nona is somewhat heavy for sustained use.

Norse Paddle Co.
P.O. Box 77
Pine Grove Mills, Pennsylvania 16868
Possibly the strongest white-water paddle made, the Norse has a fiberglass-covered aluminum shaft with dynel-covered fiberglass blade and riveted aluminum tip. Not indestructible, but very strong.

Old Town Canoe Co., Inc.
Old Town, Maine 04468
Old Town has fine quality Maine guide-style paddles in ash, maple, and spruce.

Sawyer Canoe Co., Inc.
8891 Rogue River Highway
Rogue River, Oregon 97537
Sawyer makes paddles of varying styles and materials. Best known is their fiberglass and wood cruising model. The Kruger Perma Paddle shown in figure

15 is built entirely of fiberglass and weighs only 23 ounces. Sawyer paddles are well known for their extreme lightness.

Seda Products
P.O. Box 41B
San Ysidro, California 92073
Seda makes paddles with both wood and fiberglass blades. Fiberglass paddles have vaulting pole shafts and strong plastic T-grips. All Seda paddles are built to take it and are excellent for tough white-water use.

Smoker Lumber Co., Inc.
Box 65
New Paris, Indiana 46553
All-wood paddles in various styles are offered by Smoker. Paddles are decently made and reasonably strong.

Sports Equipment, Inc.
10465 SR 44
Mantua, Ohio 44255
This company carries a very strong, reasonably priced paddle with plastic-covered aluminum shaft and reinforced fiberglass blade, though it is somewhat heavy.

Voyageur Trophy
Voyageur Company, Inc.
Box 202M, Cape Cottage Branch
Cape Elizabeth, Maine 04017
A nicely made, traditionally designed, all-ash paddle, similar to Old Town and L. L. Bean guide paddles, this one can be personally monogrammed.

Wonacott Canoes, Inc.
P.O. Box 1902
Wenatchee, Washington 98801
A linseed-oil treated, laminated cherry wood paddle, the Wonacott is of very high quality.

Index

About the Author

Cliff Jacobson, veteran canoeist, has traveled many of North America's rivers and has led numerous group canoe trips, especially with teen-agers. His most recent canoe trip was to James Bay in Canada's north. He has been a forester with the U.S. Bureau of Land Management, is an expert rifleman, and now teaches environmental science in junior high school. His articles have appeared in many outdoor sport and environmental magazines. He lives in Hastings, Minnesota, with his wife and two young daughters.